PANDORA PRESS

WORKING YOUR WAY TO THE BOTTOM

Hilda Scott was born in New York City and attended the Fieldston School and Vassar College. Following graduation she worked for some years for *Time* and *Life* magazines. The next thirty years were spent living and working as a writer and journalist in Eastern and Western Europe. Her first book (1974), *Does Socialism Liberate Women?* (Beacon Press) (British title, *Women and Socialism* (Allison & Busby)) was the result of prolonged residence in Czechoslovakia where she brought up two children and experienced at first hand the trials of the working mother in a country committed to socialist planning. The search for an alternative solution to women's subordination took her on several study visits to Sweden. Her findings were published (1982) in *Sweden's 'Right to be Human'*, written while she was living in Austria where she also had an opportunity to learn something about women and development in the Third World through her contact with women at the United Nations Industrial Development Organization (UNIDO) headquarters in Vienna. Her main interest for the past decade has been the comparative study of women in different types of industrial society. Her articles on women's position have appeared in journals in North America and Europe and she is also a member of the editorial advisory board of *Women's Studies International Forum*. She returned to the US permanently in 1980 and now lives in Cambridge, Massachusetts.

Cover Illustrator: Christine Roche.

D0096909

WORKING YOUR WAY TO THE BOTTOM
The feminization of poverty

Hilda Scott

PANDORA PRESS

London, Boston, Melbourne and Henley

First published in 1984 by Pandora Press
(Routledge & Kegan Paul plc)

14 Leicester Square, London WC2H 7PH, England

9 Park Street, Boston, Mass. 02108, USA

464 St Kilda Road, Melbourne,
Victoria 3004, Australia and

Broadway House, Newtown Road,
Henley-on-Thames, Oxon RG9 1EN, England

Photoset in 10 on 11½ pt Century Schoolbook
by Kelly Typesetting Ltd, Bradford-on-Avon, Wiltshire
and printed in Great Britain
by The Guernsey Press

Library of Congress Cataloging in Publication Data

Scott, Hilda, 1915–

Working your way to the bottom.
Bibliography: p.
Includes index.
1. Sex discrimination in employment. 2. Sex
discrimination against women. 3. Women heads of households.
4. Poverty. I. Title.
HD6060.S39 1984   331.4   84–15913

British Library CIP data available

ISBN 0–86358–011–4

CONTENTS

PREFACE

It is no news that the problem of poverty is increasing in urgency. It is endemic in the Third World. Differences between the rich and poor countries are widening. The welfare states have not closed the gap between their own poor and rich. On the day I finished this book the results of a study funded by thirteen private groups and foundations were published showing that hunger has reached 'epidemic proportions' in the United States and is growing rapidly. Attacks on welfare spending and unemployment are increasing the ranks of the poor, and special terminology has been coined to classify them. We now have, in addition to the old poor, the 'new poor': members of the middle class who have never stood in line at soup kitchens before; and the 'permanently poor': people who have never or rarely been employed, or work in low-paid, dead-end jobs with no prospects of escape from the trap.

What is much less generally recognized is the increasing extent to which women are represented among the world's poor. 'The feminization of poverty' is the phrase used to describe the fact that a growing proportion of families below the official poverty line are headed by women alone. It is seen as one of several manifestations of the economic hardship caused by recession and cuts in public spending. The treatment most frequently prescribed is the expansion of public assistance to poor mothers and children, and the provision of training that will enable women without skills to become better providers.

In spite of the attention to the problems of poor women in the press, by public agencies, and even by some politicians, it frequently proves necessary to defend the very concept of the feminization of poverty from attacks on both the right and the left. Often these overlap in a curious way. Women's poverty, it is argued by the right, is due to the instability of the family (often, specifically, the black family) and a pervasive moral laxness that produces teenage pregnancies and children born outside marriage. On the left it is held that to talk about the feminization of poverty is to divert attention from issues of class and race, that women's poverty cannot be discussed separately from men's poverty. What I hear both sides saying is that there is nothing wrong with women that an employed husband could not cure.

This book says that far from being the temporary problem of a special category of particularly underprivileged women, what has been diagnosed so far is the most visible symptom of a threat that hangs over the majority of women of the world. It is my argument that women's share in poverty worldwide is increasing and will continue to increase even if there is an economic upswing.

Many years of study of the position of women in Eastern and Western Europe have convinced me that the position of women throughout the industrialized countries is more alike than it is different. This is true for the countries that call themselves socialist, for the most committed of the welfare states, and for militantly free enterprise countries like the US. It is the result of a model of 'progress' that places increasing economic responsibilities on women without redefining their role as the mainstay of family life in the home. By transposing this model onto the very different cultural patterns of the Third World, together with the conditions that produced it, we have helped to create extreme distortions in women's lives on the rest of the globe.

Despite the success stories about women who are on the road to making it in a man's world with which the media bombard us, and despite the food and fashion advertising directed at the new management woman, most of us know that not everyone who wears an executive suit sits in an executive suite or ever will. Overall, women's position in the industrialized countries is precarious. At a conference at Cornell University in October 1983 held in honor of the 80th birthday of Alice Cook (pioneer in establishing the study of women in industry as a subject worthy of academic attention), Marion Janjic of the International Labor Organization in Geneva said:

> If I had to sum up . . . I would say that never in the history of the women's movement has there been such an elaborated and equalitarian set of institutions to promote their rights. In spite of this, because of the economic recession on the one hand, and of the technological revolution and the unbalanced economic growth between the North and the South on the other, women's position is at the same time very fragile.

Speakers from Western Europe confirmed that although their countries are bound by a triad of obligations – the ILO Convention on Equal Pay, binding directives of the European Economic Community and constitutional and legislative changes in individual countries – the net effect on discrimination is close to zero because of the way laws and directives are written, interpreted and enforced. This is compounded by lack of effective support from unions and the hostility or indifference of male workers and employers.

Sociological literature offers us packaged explanations to the effect that poverty is influenced by class, race, nation, economic region, ethnic group and gender. This is an ideologically impeccable conclusion that can never get you into trouble but also does not leave you much the wiser. In fact, considerable academic research has been done on the role of the first five factors in determining who is poor; the sixth is a recent afterthought. Yet gender cuts across all the others. Women are poorer than men in all the first five categories. Surely this says something about the power of gender as a way of getting a handle on the whole issue of poverty.

In choosing to look at poverty as it is determined by gender I do not deny the importance of other factors. I believe that by concentrating on the reasons why women are especially at risk will give us a way of getting a fresh perspective on poverty as a whole. It makes use of the power of 'defamiliarization,' or to put it another way, it helps us to see the given as ungiven, to borrow a phrase from the Canadian sociologist Thelma MacCormack.

Some of the givens such an approach calls into question are our conventional definitions of poverty, class, work and value. This was brought home to me when a UN report on the status of women in 1979 declared that women do two-thirds of the world's work and receive 10 per cent of the world's income. When I accepted a redefinition of work that included unpaid work and assumed that all income was payment for work done, I realizd that men were getting paid at a rate eighteen times that of women. That was enough to convince me that the economic positions of women and men were qualitatively different, and that the treatment could not be reduced to equal pay and better social benefits.

While women throughout the world are increasingly becoming economically responsible for their children, the income gap between men and women is growing. Long-run trends are that job segregation by gender will also increase; so will the gap between women's training and the demands of technology; so will women's share in the 'secondary' (dead-end) jobs as opposed to the 'primary' jobs. Difficult as the situation of the majority of people in the Third World is, the position of women is still deteriorating with respect to that of men. What all women have in common is that they share most of the unpaid work of the world.

Woman's unpaid work, her productive and reproductive labor for which she receives no remuneration, underpins the world's economy, yet it is peripheral to the world's economy as men define it, and therefore has no value. It is this that makes women a category of persons who are economically invisible, whose work is non-work, who have no experience or skills, who don't need a regular income because their husband supports them.

How did men come to be the ones who define work and value? Is there something eternal and scientific about these definitions? Are they based on a 'natural' division of tasks between women and men? Do women have different definitions than men, and how might work and value be defined in a non-sexist society? In documenting my arguments and suggesting answers to these questions I rely heavily (though not entirely) on recent research by feminist scholars and writers. Without the women's movement and the intellectual ferment generated by it, we would never have become aware of some of the ways the documentation of social problems has been skewed or the extent to which the categories used to analyze them have blinded us to reality.

It is a truism that if you ask the wrong questions you get the wrong answers. In the past decade or so women have started to ask some questions that were never asked before, based on their own experience. Many traditionally defined concepts were found to be useless in illuminating that experience. No one claims that all the answers have now been discovered, but there is no doubt that the search has already affected the way all of us see the world.

My feminist bias does not lead me to want to share poverty equally between women and men. Neither is my conclusion wholly pessimistic. It is that new definitions of poverty, of class, of work and of value can help us conceptualize a world that makes constructive use of the fact that opportunities for paid work are permanently on the decline while the importance of unpaid work has never been so plain. The belief that all unpaid work is destined to be absorbed into paid labor and that such a transformation would be a good thing is, I think, a long-held misconception that feminist research is helping us to overcome. We need to establish unpaid work as a legitimate economic category, with its own criteria of value and its own rewards for both women and men because the already visible alternative is mass unemployment and the sloughing-off of welfare programs on women family members and volunteers on the pretext of 'returning them to the community' as the state finds the costs increasingly prohibitive.

One aim of this book is to engage women for concrete thinking about the future. There is an encouraging trend in future research that emphasizes peace, equality of opportunity, better distribution of wealth and concern for the environment but it still assumes male models of society. We need to create our own blueprints if we want the future to incorporate 'female' values in a way that the past has not.

In acknowledging my debt to several hundred thinkers, including many whom I have not actually cited in this work, I take full responsibility for the conclusions drawn. I use this opportunity to thank those who called my attention to literature I would otherwise have missed: Jean Bethke Elshtain, Anne Fausto-Sterling, Penny Gill, Hilda Kahne, Felicia Lamport, Andrew Lass, Herbert Lass, Joan Rothschild, Ann Scott, Angela and Michael Simmons, Dorothy Sterling, Martha Tolpin, Susan Woodward, Elizabeth Wilson. Special thanks are due to Penny Gill, Andrew Lass and Ann Scott for their critical comments on parts of the manuscript. Finally, I am grateful to my editors, Philippa Brewster and Dale Spender, for the stimulation and encouragement they provided.

Cambridge, Massachusetts
April 1984

Chapter 1

WHAT IS POVERTY?

Elaine Cleveland, 43, mother of ten children, 'took her family off welfare.' The family had begun to receive benefits in 1974 when Walter Cleveland, a tenant farmer in upstate New York, had fallen ill with an inoperable tumor and had become progressively less able to work. Even before that they had been 'achingly poor.'

Ultimately unable to stand the indignities she and the children suffered as welfare recipients, Elaine went out to work. Even with two jobs – as a waitress and a nursing home attendant – she made less than the approximately $1000 monthly the family had received in welfare payments. Although she had only nine years of schooling, she determined to become a licensed practical nurse, and with the aid of government loans, a scholarship and financial aid from her church, she completed the training course and found a job at Sullivan County General Hospital. She plans to continue her studies and eventually to become a registered nurse.

Life gave this story nine pages of text and pictures in its June 1982 issue under the headline, 'How One Family Broke the Poverty Circle.' Behind the obvious American moral of this story (no matter what the odds the person with guts will win out) there are several other messages.

Poverty is again officially visible. That is the first message. It has not been reduced to 'core poverty,' or 'case poverty.' It can happen to anyone, to 'ordinary people' – white, intelligent, resourceful, good-looking; the statistics are there. In the world's first industrial power, the US, during 1981, 2.2 million people joined the ranks of the official poor, increasing their number to nearly 32 million, or 14 per cent of the population. In 1982 another 4 million were added to the rolls, returning America's poverty rate to 15 per cent, the highest figure since President Lyndon Johnson launched the Great Society in 1965.

The second message is that poverty is women's business. The burden of raising the Cleveland family from the aching poverty they experienced as farmers and the shameful poverty they endured on relief to the more respectable status of a low-income family was picked up by a woman. This is not only acceptable; it is an example to all of us. Of course women have been doing this since time immemorial, but in our part of the world and in our century at least it has not been held up as a model solution.

In fact, just twenty years ago, when poverty surfaced in the midst of affluence in our Western societies and was found not to be 'an afterthought' (Galbraith, 1958, p. 323) but a mass affliction, it was still considered a male problem and its core was the inability of a man to support his family. As Michael Harrington (1969) wrote first in 1962, in a book that is credited with directly influencing the US government's decision to launch an anti-poverty program, *The Other America*, if family incomes had grown since the Great Depression of the 1930s, it was because more wives were working. The costs of this progress were not negligible, however: 'A tremendous growth in the number of working wives is an expensive way to increase incomes. It will be paid for in terms of the impoverishment of home life . . .' (p. 179).

The same point was made by Dwight Macdonald in an influential article in *The New Yorker* called 'Our Invisible Poor' (1963), in which he reviewed Harrington's book. He deplored the fact that 4 million American mothers of pre-school children were working in the face of almost total absence of day care facilities, and declared the neglect of children the price of improved national statistics on poverty.

Today it is the rule rather than the exception throughout the industrialized world for mothers of dependent children to be working outside the home although, with the possible exception of the German Democratic Republic, France and Belgium, no country comes near meeting the demand for day care. In Britain, for example, it has been estimated that the number of families in poverty would triple if wives ceased to work (Glucklich and Snell, 1982).

Poverty is becoming more visible in the 1980s because it is more widespread, and women are becoming a more visible part of the poor because in fact a process of 'feminization of poverty' is taking place. While women have kept the increasing number of two-earner families from falling into poverty they have also become the sole earner in an increasing number of families with dependent children. In the US the number of one-parent families nearly doubled between 1970 and 1981; in Great Britain their total grew by two-thirds. Yet few women earn enough to support a family.

'Feminization of poverty' is a phrase used chiefly to describe the economic vulnerability of women who are the sole support of their children. Actually its implications are much broader. In this book it will be used to refer to the whole complex of forces that keep women in an economically precarious situation – considerably more precarious than that of most men – while increasing their economic responsibilities.

Underpinning this complex is the fact that the vast majority of women are poor in the absolute sense that they carry out an enormous amount of indispensable work without any remuneration whatsoever. According to International Labor Organization data, 90 per cent of the unpaid work of the world is done by women (Dauber and Cain, 1981). To encompass the real economic position of women, we would need a new definition of poverty. Such a definition would help us to understand an important mechanism that contributes to maintaining poverty on a world scale, the mind-boggling and soul-destroying polarization between those who have control over resources and those who do not, within countries and among countries.

But first let us look at how poverty is defined in the modern world.

How do we know, for example, that Elaine Cleveland has 'broken the poverty circle?' If she no longer receives welfare checks but the actual family income is lower than it was, is she more or less poor, and if she climbs slightly above the 'poverty line' is she no longer poor?

It's apparently easy to identify the rich, as in a famous

exchange between F. Scott Fitzgerald and Ernest Hemingway:

> *Fitzgerald*: 'The rich are different from us.'
> *Hemingway:* 'Yes, they have more money.'

But the poor: they have less money, but how much less? Is it only a question of money?

Attempts to quantify poverty have proliferated in the past two decades. Poverty, like most of our eternal-sounding concepts, has a changing content. All writers today distinguish between absolute and relative poverty. They agree that 'starvation, death from exposure, and loss of life due to some other total lack of resources are the only absolute forms of poverty' (Valentine, 1968, p. 12), and that in high-income societies pure physical survival is not the main issue.

Even when President Franklin D. Roosevelt made his famous 'One-Third of a Nation' Inaugural Address in 1937 ('I see one-third of a nation ill-housed, ill-clad, ill-nourished') he was not using criteria that might be applied to the starving poor of Asia but comparing the condition of masses of American poor in the Depression to the norm then considered acceptable. For most people and governments in the industrialized world poverty means not having 'basic necessities,' but what are they? The words of Adam Smith in *The Wealth of Nations* (1776) are most often quoted:

> By necessaries I understand not only the commodities which are indispensably necessary for the support of life, but whatever the custom of the century renders it indecent for creditable people, even of the lowest order, to be without.' (1937, p. 821)

The most important early British study adopting this approach, made by Seebohn Rowntree in 1899, illustrates the temporal quality of necessities. Rowntree specified as necessary clothing for a young woman of that year: 'one pair of boots, two aprons, one second-hand dress, one skirt made from an old dress, a third of the cost of a new hat, a third the cost of a shawl and a jacket, two pair of stockings, a few unspecified underclothes, one pair of stays and one pair of old boots worn as slippers' (Townsend, 1979, p. 50).

In 1899 a poor woman could have been identified any-where by her shabby clothes. Travelling through America in the early 1960s, Michael Harrington (1969) found that one reason the poor were invisible was that they no longer wore the stereotyped rags and hand-me-downs of the destitute. Thanks to mass-produced clothing, 'there are tens of thousands of Americans in the big cities who are wearing shoes, perhaps even a stylishly cut suit or dress, and yet are hungry' (p. 5). He also found people with TV sets, cars and telephones who were hungry.

But the 'new' poverty of the 1960s differed from the 'old' pre-World War II poverty in a much more general way. The New Deal in the US, the beginning of the welfare state in other countries, and most of all the industrial expansion that followed the war, had raised the living standard of a substantial part of the population. In time, it was confidently believed, this would be true for everyone.

Economic justice was not an issue in the 1950's, for there was confidence that all in society, especially those at the bottom, were benefiting from expansion. The bigger economic pie was yielding relatively larger slices to the bottommost groups. Social problems were interpreted as gracefully succumbing to the mighty power of economic growth.' (Miller and Roby, 1970, p. 4)

As Piven and Cloward (1982) point out, the sheer extent of unemployment and misery in the 1930s helped to break down the idea that economic misfortune was visited on those who deserved it. As many members of the upper and middle classes went from riches to rags overnight, the cause had to be external and not character flaws inherent in the poor. Poverty uncovered in the years of economic expansion was more selective. It affected people who had fallen through the safety net of welfare legislation. The poor were those whom the boom had passed by. They were the people who, to use Harrington's expression, were 'upside down in the economy' (1969, p. 12). For them the technological revolution had meant worse jobs because they lacked skills and the means to acquire new ones; or big agriculture had meant hunger because they had been small farmers. The majority of the poor were concentrated in urban ghettos or in rural areas that suburban commuters did not get to see as they travelled the highways.

Yet they could not be dismissed as case histories – ill, poorly educated, drop-outs, alcoholics – or minority groups, or pockets of poverty. Using one-half of the Bureau of Labor Statistics' 'modest but adequate family budget' as his standard, Harrington estimated that there were close to 50 million Americans who, for reasons which he located primarily in their environment, had not had the same chance as others. Other 'experts' arrived at more conservative figures, but they were forced to recognize that poverty existed to an unexpected degree.

In Britain, too, poverty had increased in spite of comprehensive income maintenance schemes undertaken in the 1940s. A study reported by Townsend (1979) found 7.5 million people out of a population of 52 million living in low-income households in 1960, or more than 14 per cent of the population, compared with 8 per cent in 1953–4.

When in 1965 President Johnson declared his 'War on Poverty' there was very little research available to guide the government in distinguishing the really poor from the not-so-poor. Britain already had its definition of need, incorporated in the Beveridge Plan of 1942, designed to raise the alarmingly low levels of nutrition, health and housing uncovered during World War II. Lord Beveridge had borrowed it from Seebohn Rowntree who in 1899 had arrived at a poverty line using as a subsistence standard the minimum necessities needed for 'the maintenance of physical efficiency' (Townsend, 1979).

This idea of poverty as a condition in which people are unable to obtain the basic necessities of life, understood in a relative sense, has become the almost universal criterion according to which poverty is measured in the industrialized countries, from Austria to the United States. According to the International Labor Organization, in 1967 44 of the 61 countries then surveyed were administering public assistance schemes paying cash allowances according to a means test. Poverty is calculated relative to social norms of minimum necessary consumption, and is usually adjusted from time to time to meet changes in the price index.

Predictably, government bodies responsible for spending money try to arrive at the lowest possible figure for 'necessary consumption.' Mollie Orshansky, who developed the US poverty line at the Social Security Administration, relates that the SSA had proposed two measures of need. One, based on a 'low-cost' diet developed by the Bureau of Labor Statistics, would have put the minimum necessary income in 1962 for a non-farm family of four at nearly $4000 annually. Using the 'economy' diet of the Department of Agriculture, however, the same family could get along on slightly more than $3000. Obviously many more Americans would turn out to be poor and eligible for assistance if the higher income were used as the poverty line. And indeed, the Office of Economic Opportunity and the Council of Economic Advisors selected the lower one as a 'working tool.' 'It is interesting,' Orshansky recalled later, 'that few outside the Social Security Administration ever wanted to talk about the higher measure. Everybody wanted only to talk about the lower one . . .' (Miller and Roby, 1970, p. 8).

That isn't the only thing wrong with this kind of measure of relative poverty, however. How inadequate it is we can discover for ourselves by reviewing the way it is calculated in the US.

The basis for the calculation of the US poverty line is the Department of Agriculture's economy food plan of 1961, using the recommended daily allowances of the National Research Council of the National Academy of Sciences and actual family spending patterns at different income levels. Since there are no acceptable definitions of minimum acceptable housing or other non-food expenditures like clothing and furniture, the total poverty line budget is arrived at by multiplying the food costs by three. This is because Americans spent one-third of their after-tax income on food, according to the 1955 Household Food Consumption Survey. Using these figures as guides, 124 separate poverty income ceilings were arrived at for different types of families, since family requirements differ according to size, number of children, their age, the sex of the breadwinner, the area of residence, and whether the family is farm or urban. The resulting poverty line, or what is really a band of poverty lines, is brought up to date each year in accordance with changes in the cost of living as reflected in the Consumer Price Index.

As will immediately be seen, what was intended to be a relative measure of poverty has become an absolute one. Poor Americans are still expected to eat what Americans were eating twenty-five years ago, in spite of the fact that food customs and 'needs' have changed more decisively than in any previous period.

Further, while all other family expenditures (rent, heating, clothing, etc.) in the poverty line budget are still arrived at by multiplying the food costs by three, Americans now typically spend much less than one-third of their income on food. In fact, a study mandated by Congress in 1974 and carried out by a task force established by the Assistant Secretary for Education, *The Measure of Poverty* (US Department of Health, Education, and Welfare, 1976), admitted that the figure was closer to one-fifth.

The third factor that makes this measure obsolete is that US incomes have increased faster than the Consumer Price Index has risen. Between 1959 and 1969 alone, the average income of a four-member family rose 37 per cent, but the poverty line moved up only 9 per cent. Many people who had become poor by relative standards were thus not counted. Since 1968 the US Census Bureau has been publishing data on families in poverty using the measure worked out in 1964, and politicians have pointed happily to the progress made in overcoming poverty. According to government figures, the number of people in poverty declined from 28 million in 1966 to 24 million in 1977, from 14.7 per cent of the population to 11.6 per cent.

These figures have little to do with reality. If only slight adjustments had been made in the 1970s to bring the method of calculation more in line with actual spending patterns, 15 million people would have been plunged into official poverty at the stroke of a computer. This would have happened if the Department of Agriculture's 'economy food plan' had been replaced in the calculations by its more up-to-date 'thrifty plan,' which incorporated new nutrition standards and food preferences while still remaining below the amount 90 per cent of Americans spend on food, and if the multiplier used to allow for expenditures on non-foods had been raised modestly from 3 to 3.4. The task force's report notes:

It is evident that many critical judgements significantly affect the level of the current poverty lines. . . . To understand how significant these judgements can be, one need only consider the implications of using the low-cost food plan rather than the economy food plan and using a 5:1 rather than a 3:1 multiplier. These two changes, both within the range of reasonable judgement and based on statistical interpretations, would *more than double the official poverty thresholds and include about one-third of the population as poor.*' (p. 75) (my italics – H.S.)

Thus the present figure of 15 per cent of Americans judged to be officially poor in 1982 – a statistic that every commentator finds shockingly high – is ridiculously low. People in the US don't believe that a family of four can get along on an income of $9800, the 1982 poverty line for a family that size; they put the minimum at an average of $15,400, according to a Gallup Poll inquiry in January 1983. By coincidence, this is almost exactly the US Bureau of Labor Statistics' own 'lower standard of living' threshold. By this standard, not 34.4 million people but 55–60 million people in the US can be considered poor.

It would seem that nothing more need be said about the subjective character of poverty measurements, the arbitrary way in which indicators are chosen, the lack of independent criteria, and the haphazard character of decisions that affect the lives and economic conditions of millions. The difference between poverty which entitles one to assistance, and non-poverty, which does not, can be whether it is considered politically expedient to recognize an updated measure. The US has decided to stick with the old one.

Townsend (1979) has characterized the US method of calculating poverty as 'static and historically barren' (p. 36), which seems like an understatement. Similar methods of measuring relative poverty in other prosperous countries could undoubtedly be shown to produce the same kind of anomalies and inconsistencies. The state's subsistence standard is an administrative construct and there is nothing scientific or objective about it. It stands between us and a clear view of what is really going on.

Understandably, governments having missed the mark so badly, there was an outpouring of literature in the late 1960s and early 1970s by social scientists seeking for definitions that would capture the essential character of poverty in societies where luxury spending was becoming a necessity for so many.

Casting around for a better way to define poverty, many investigators concluded that the term poverty itself was inadequate to describe the kind of exclusion and social inferiority experienced by low-income families in highly industrialized societies.

For many, Richard Titmuss of the London School of Economics had provided guideposts when, in his book *Income Distribution and Social Change* (1962) he painstakingly dismantled the statistics and methods of the Board of Inland Revenue and punctured the widely held myth that there had been a substantial redistribution of income in British society since the end of World War II. 'Ancient inequalities have assumed new and more subtle forms; conventional categories are no longer adequate for the task of measuring them' he wrote (p. 199).

Titmuss pointed out that the obvious inequalities between the incomes of the poor and those of big property owners, shareholders and inheritors had been replaced by intricate relationships which the old-fashioned statistical approach of the British government was incapable of reflecting. The concept of poverty, he said, had to be placed in the context of social change, and interpreted 'in relation to the growth of more complex and specialized institutions of power, authority and privilege' (p. 187). These changes included new ways of 'getting, spending, spreading and storing income,' new benefits and privileges flowing from status, and new special concessions to certain groups to encourage efficiency, investment, professional self-improvement and 'other socially approved objectives' (pp. 190–1).

Other authors spelled this out: if poverty was to be seen

as relative, then the poor were poor in comparison with the rest of the population not only in current cash income but in terms of their long-term financial prospects and their access to better jobs, education, status and political power (Griffin, 1978; Townsend, 1979; Valentine, 1968). *'Social poverty* implies ... a relationship of inferiority, dependence or exploitation,' in Eric Hobsbawm's definition (1968, p. 398). *'Poverty* has become the acceptable way of discussing the more disturbing issue of inequality,' wrote Miller and Roby (1970, p. 3).

In their analysis of inequality, these last authors offered six dimensions of well-being, and argued that to eliminate poverty the US government would have to strive for a better distribution of all of them:

1 income, including income mobility and non-monetary benefits from pensions and stock options;
2 assets, such as savings and property;
3 basic services: access to health, protection, neighborhood amenities, social services and transportation;
4 self-respect: what discriminatory barriers have to be overcome;
5 opportunities for education;
6 participation in many forms of decision making.

In the UK Peter Townsend (1979) had developed the concept of 'relative deprivation' along similar lines. People suffering from relative deprivation were 'deprived of the conditions of life which ordinarily define membership of society. If they lack or are denied resources to obtain access to these conditions of life and so fulfil membership of society, they are in poverty' (p. 915).

Townsend hypothesized that there was a cut-off point on the income scale below which this kind of deprivation increased disproportionately. People who fell below this point could be considered poor. In 1968–9 he and his co-workers devised sixty 'style of living' indicators and collected information from 2000 representative UK households. Using a 39-page questionnaire, they not only recorded incomes but interviewed families on the quality of their meals, their clothing, utilities, housing, working conditions and benefits, health, education, neighborhoods, and their recreation and social life.

According to the results of this survey, the investigators concluded that in 1968–9 26 per cent of the population was living in 'relative deprivation.' However, as much as 35 per cent of the sample experienced this level of poverty at some time during the year and, Townsend concluded in his monumental 1200-page discussion of the study (1979), more than half the population of the UK experiences poverty or near-poverty at some time in the life cycle. 'Poverty,' he wrote, 'is a national phenomenon which is structurally pervasive and of major dimensions' (p. 913).

If this was true when Townsend made his survey, it is surely even more so in today's Great Britain, judging from the government's own conservative figures. During Mrs Thatcher's first two years as prime minister (1979–81), the number of people 'on the margins of poverty' rose from 11.5 to 15 million, or one person in four, according to the Department of Health and Social Security; those actually below the poverty line increased from 6 to 9 million, to reach 17 per cent of the population (higher than the 1960 figure) (*Guardian*, 28 February 1983; *Manchester Guardian Weekly*, 6 November 1983). Cuts in the value of unemployment, sickness, maternity and other benefits, reductions in the number of free school meals and in school transportation, the increase in the tax burden on low-income families, and the failure of the lowest wages and of pensions to keep pace with prices all compound the desperation caused by record unemployment.

The chief lesson of the foregoing is that there are no fixed or objective measures of poverty either in the 'subsistence' sense or in the sense of 'inequality' or 'relative deprivation.' Governments' strictly drawn poverty lines, as we have shown above, are not based on any rigorous investigation of need, on any consistent standard with relation to the non-poor population, but on political judgements using arbitrarily selected data that is, moreover, out of date. As we have seen in the case of the US, the resulting 'line' can be 100 per cent off its course. This is hardly a measure of poverty to be taken seriously.

Attempts to devise measurements that truly reflect changing social needs, including needs 'that have traditionally been excluded from consideration in devising poverty standards' (Townsend, 1979, p. 915), also depend on subjective judgements about appropriate indicators. It could hardly be otherwise, and that is not the major problem with this approach.

It advances our understanding of poverty to have it described not as a set of symptoms diagnosed in certain kinds of people (those suffering from ill health, old age, dark skin), but as the result of the mechanisms that govern the distribution of national wealth so that certain people are *a priori* excluded from the race. ('*Not only the poor but the entire society is at issue today*' [Miller and Roby, 1970, p. 5]).

It is a step forward to define poverty in terms of access to resources which are not just family income but assets, status at work and in the community, and involvement in decision making. This new approach has a built-in blind spot, however, because it, like the poverty line based on annual income alone, uses the family as the unit of analysis.

If poverty is about control over resources in the broad sense of the term, and reflects 'access of various groups to sources of economic and political power' (Griffin, 1978, p. 135), then, as the people with the least control over resources, those most likely to be poor are women. At present in the US one-half of all gainfully employed women are already either supporting themselves or are the sole support of a family, and this is a pattern developing in all industrialized lands (Merritt, 1982). Any married woman from a family of average assets (who does not inherit a substantial estate or receive a generous divorce settlement) will find herself dependent on her own access to resources if she loses her husband. Minority women are doubly at risk, elderly minority women triply so. What justifies us, then, in defining a married woman in terms of her husband's assets, opportunities and status?

This family-based way of counting the poor, which everyone seems to take for granted, disguises what really goes on in society. Like most policies that affect the family, it is based on the false assumption that there is a natural and eternal division of work in this world between women and men, that women take care of the home free and in return can count on the financial support of a man.

Townsend (1979) hints at this problem but passes it by:

> Many people, and overwhelmingly married women and children, are not in poverty by virtue of any *personal* characteristics so much as indirectly by virtue of the labour market, wage or social security characteristics of the principle income recipient of the family unit. (p. 899)

It is not just a question, he says, of how incomes come to be graded or resources distributed, but how access is decided and why access to resources is restricted for certain types of dependents. He perceives that it depends on how society views marriage, the family, and unpaid work, but there he leaves it. The sequel is, however, that many people who are 'indirectly' *not* in poverty by virtue of the chief breadwinner's status *are* poor in the sense that their own access to resources is limited.

What does the poverty we have been talking about, poverty that is compatible with owning a TV set and even an automobile, poverty that has access to monthly cash welfare benefits that can far exceed the average annual income of an African family, have in common with the poverty we know to be the style of life in the Third World? Can there be a valid woman-centered view of this poverty, or should we retreat before the words of one Third World woman delegate to the Forum held in Copenhagen in 1980 during the UN Conference of the United Nations Decade for Women: 'To talk feminism to a woman who has no water, no food and no home is nonsense'!

This book will argue that it is impossible to attack the problem of poverty in the industrialized or the developing world effectively unless the extent to which poverty is a women's problem is recognized. This is not to underestimate the importance of class, race, national and international divisions. The fact is that feminist research during the past twenty years has revealed that all these divisions affect women in special ways, ways that have been largely ignored. This is true regardless of the differences between the issues that Western women and Third World women put at the top of their lists at any given time, or of the way they perceive their own and each other's lives.

It is not just a question of social justice, or of failing to make use of the creative abilities of one-half of humanity, although these frequently raised arguments for recognizing that women have the same worth as men are powerful. Women's poverty is an increasing part of world poverty. It is a special kind of poverty whose causes are not fully understood, that are in fact still largely invisible to most males engaged in official and unofficial poverty research. Until poverty is at least seen for what it is, it cannot be treated.

Chapter 2

WOMEN WORK THEIR WAY TO THE BOTTOM

Having seen how currently used official measures of poverty are improvized, and how far we are from having a usable alternative, it is a temptation to devise a measure of our own, based on the concept described in the last chapter that equates poverty with inequality and a sense of deprivation.

The first step would be to question a representative sample of women and men, as individuals, concerning their current income, job prospects, assets, income mobility, education and training, status in the community, and share in decision making. We would then assign scores to their answers, ask the computer to work out their 'equality coefficient' and compare it, say, to 50 per cent of the mean for both sexes. My hypothesis is that a substantial majority of women would fall below this 'poverty line.' My poverty index would be hotly rejected by those who are used to calculating the well-being of women in terms of men, but it would provide a much more reliable picture of the actual economic position of the population than anything we are using now.

Another much simpler measure, more in keeping with government methods, would be to adopt the stance that to be considered 'not poor' an adult should be able to support herself/himself and one dependent (to allow for the care of children, the elderly and the disabled). This is not a completely far-fetched idea. There is a precedent set by the Swedish government which, as early as 1968, declared it the aim of all legislation and social policy to encourage the economic independence of every adult, to support a shift from man-the-breadwinner and woman-the-homemaker to a society of self-sufficient individuals (H. Scott, 1982a).

In the US in 1980 half the women of working age were in the labor force, but only about half of them earned more than the minimum necessary to keep a family of two above the poverty line. This means that some 75 per cent of all American women aged 16 to 64 would be dependent on resources other than their own earned income if they had to support themselves and one other person.

To complete this study we would need another survey to determine what proportion of women have adequate assets in their own name, or can count on being cared for financially in case of their husband's death. The difference would give us the percentage of women of working age living in (official) poverty or 'in risk' of poverty. My conservative guess is that it would be well over 50 per cent, and this without making any adjustments in the admittedly conservatively drawn US poverty line.

Some will object that I am not distinguishing sufficiently between poor working-class women and middle-class women who, by definition, are better off. In fact, what I am trying to do is to distinguish the real stratification of women more precisely. In conventional studies, 'working-class' and 'middle-class' women are pigeon-holed according to the occupation of their husband regardless of what they themselves do, with disorienting results.

Joan Acker (1973), in a classic study, takes apart the smug assumptions about women's social status that pervade sociological stratification literature. The fundamental precepts are, of course, that the family is the unit in the stratification system, that the family's position is determined by the male head, and that females derive their status from the male to whom they are attached. Acker punctures these related propositions by pointing out that as early as 1960 40 per cent of US households were not male-headed; either they were headed by a woman, or consisted of a woman alone, or of husband-and-wife families in which the husband was not in the labor force or worked part-time. She points out how inconsistent it is to rank an unmarried woman by her education and occupation and then forget all about it when she marries, and she adds that 'once we question that the woman's status is determined by the man, we must also question the assumption that the status of the female is equal to that of her male' (p. 177).

Are secretaries, nurses or teachers working-class if they are married to a man who works on an assembly line but middle-class if the man is an accountant? Do these jobs confer middle-class occupational status even though the rewards are less than many working-class occupations command? 'Working-class,' especially in Marxist analysis, usually refers to someone engaged directly in production, in work productive of new values. A number of authors have pointed out that relatively few gainfully employed women actually work in manufacturing (throughout the industrialized West the figure rarely climbs above 20 per cent). The great female categories – clerical work, services and sales – pay less than most male workers earn; they are monotonous and low-skilled – and this is where most 'middle-class' as well as 'working-class' women end up (Eisenstein, 1982; West, 1978). Isn't it time, Jackie West (1978) asks, to take a longer look at the 'proletarianization' of part of the non-proletariat? And where does housework locate a woman in the social hierarchy, whether she does it full-time or together with a paid job?

The slippery downward slope that awaits the nominally middle-class woman when she loses her husband through separation or divorce is another side of the picture. Lee Comer (1978) comments:

> If the husband of the said middle class woman goes off with his secretary, leaving his wife to fight for maintenance for her children while she, without qualifications or even with them, struggles to find part-time work which fits in with school hours, defaults on mortgage payments, gets evicted and finally capitulates to outwork and social security (an everyday story of middle class womanhood, my mother's included), what then constitutes her fierce allegiance to the wrong side of the barricades? Or does she then have an entry card to the working class? (p. 168)

Patricia Schroeder, a member of the US Congress from Colorado who has been trying to get a legal share in men's pensions for their ex-spouses, notes that divorces of older women have skyrocketed since the introduction of no-fault divorce. Only 4 per cent of divorced wives in the US receive alimony, she says, and only 22 per cent of divorced mothers collect child support. In her experience, former wives of ambassadors can be reduced to cleaning toilets (Raspberry, 1983). The kind of insecurity that accumulates around women in the course of a lifetime breaks out like a disease in old age. Among those over 65, two-and-a-half times as many women as men live in poverty, according to Geraldine Ferraro, 1984 Democratic vice-presidential candidate. The rate for all elderly women is 20 per cent; one-half of black older women are poor! 'In risk of poverty' is not an empty phrase.

Oakley (1981) has observed that while it is true that not all women are equally oppressed, the oppression of all women lies in their dependence on the way individual men treat them. We could say by analogy that not all women are equally poor, but the special poverty of women lies in the fact that their economic position depends on their relationship with a man or their lack of it, and the provision he makes for them on death or divorce.

To get at the root of why this is so, we need to define women on the basis of their own economic characteristics, their real options, their real prospects. What are they?

Events since the beginning of the 1970s have dramatized the special vulnerability of women to poverty. Today in the US two out of three poor adults are women. The sharply increased divorce rate, the rise in teenage pregnancies, and the number of children born to unmarried mothers resulted in a 50 per cent increase in the number of all families maintained by women in the 1970s. While 15 per cent of all families are headed by women, they account for half of all the poor families in the US and they include nearly one-quarter of all children aged 3 to 13.

The feminization of poverty accounted for virtually all the growth in the official poverty rolls between 1970 and 1979; the number of poor families with mothers at the head rose by one-third, while poor male-headed families decreased by 18 per cent (Pearce and McAdoo, 1981). Many families maintained by women alone are hovering near the poverty line and would be included in any more realistic definition of poverty.

When black families are considered separately the picture is even starker. In 1981, according to the Census Bureau, one-third of the black population of the US lived below the poverty line. As many as 41 per cent of all black families are supported by women alone, and 54 per cent of these families are officially poor, compared to 27 per cent of all white families maintained by women, 16 per cent of families headed by black men, and 6 per cent of those headed by white men.

Is the trend toward 'marital instability' likely to reverse itself? Isabel Sawhill of the Urban Institute thinks not. Overall, she says (1980),

> Compared to their mothers' generation, young women today are two-and-a-half times as likely to be divorced by the time they reach their early thirties. . . . Demographers are predicting that almost one out of every three marriages among these younger couples will end in divorce at some time during their lives. (p. 202)

Poor families are not the most likely to break up. 'The higher a wife's earnings, other things being equal, the more likely it is that the couple will separate.'

This suggests that not only is the 'ideal' male-headed family on the way out, but that even the two-earner family (today the predominant form of family in the US) leads a precarious existence. In fact, since Sawhill's words were written the US divorce rate has climbed to one for every two marriages, a world record shared with Sweden and Denmark, while the Soviet Union is close behind with one divorce in every three.

At a time when poverty is growing, aid to the poor and near-poor is decreasing, in keeping with the logic that holds the poor to need less help in bad times than in good. During the 1970s, income maintenance programs, especially federally funded aid, kept many people in the US from the depths of despair (*The New York Times*, 27 July 1982). During the first two years of the Reagan presidency, 1981–2, federal income maintenance programs were cut by more than 20 billion dollars, and the poorest were hit hardest. As Piven and Cloward point out in *The New Class War* (1982):

> Non-means-tested programs such as Social Security and Medicare [health insurance for the elderly – H.S.] and a variety of veterans' benefits have been dealt with delicately and cautiously. The brunt of the cuts falls on public service employment, unemployment insurance, Medicaid [means-tested health care for the indigent – H.S.], public welfare, low-income housing subsidies, and the disability and food stamp programs. (pp. 15–19)

The largest single cash benefit program, Aid to Families with Dependent Children (AFDC), which was helping 4 million families, 93 per cent of them headed by women, was cut by 18 per cent in the fiscal 1982 budget. Four hundred thousand families were scheduled to be wiped off the rolls, and another 650,000 to have their benefits cut. The special supplemental food program for women, infants and children now reaches only 30 per cent of those potentially eligible, and 3.2 million children have been dropped from the federal school lunch program. The public service jobs program (CETA) has been eliminated and the training program decimated.

These cuts set off a wave of slashes in programs that aid low-income women: day care, temporary shelters, job training, legal aid, aid to students, and others. Many of those who administered these programs were women who now joined their clients in the ranks of the unemployed.

The poor are the targets of economy measures that destroy their fragile resources yet represent a negligible sum in comparison with the total budget. Meanwhile the well off end up better off. Columnist Ellen Goodman wrote on Mother's Day, 1981 (*Boston Globe*, 7 May):

> The proposed cuts in AFDC come to roughly $636 million. This sounds like a lot. But in Pentagon terms it's peanuts. For $614 the Pentagon can get one SSN-688 nuclear attack submarine.

The Congressional Office of the Budget, on the other hand, pointed out (*Newsweek*, 5 April 1982) that Reagan's proposed tax and spending reductions would add $15,000 to the incomes of those earning $80,000, while cutting families with earnings below $10,000 by $240.

In stressing the plight of women alone with dependent children it is not my purpose to minimize the hardship suffered by complete families in poverty. Neither is it the point to suggest that poor women in the US are any worse off than their counterparts in other industrialized countries. If, however, in the world's richest land the feminization of poverty has reached epidemic proportions and been documented on a national scale without having been diagnosed or treated by any of the relevant institutions, this does give us an insight into the magnitude of the problem.

'Worldwide,' writes Kathleen Newland (1979), 'between one-quarter and one-third of all families are supported by women; and worldwide, these families are leading candidates for poverty and hardship' (p. 153).

In Great Britain, as in the US, the 'typical' constellation of breadwinning father, housewife mother and two children under 18 accounts for only 5 per cent of all families. The number of one-parent families increased 66 per cent between 1971 and 1981 to account for one family in eight, or 12.5 per cent, not far behind the US figure. The National Council for One Parent Families disclosed in its 1981 report that one-parent families made up 58 per cent of families with children on Supplementary Benefit, the basic welfare program for low-income households, and 95 per cent of them were headed by women. While 80 per cent of lone fathers are able to rely on their own earnings, the report noted, less than half of single mothers work at all, and half of these are on part-time. As citizens of a welfare state that provides non-income-tested benefits such as health care, child allowances, sickness benefits and maternity allowances, single mothers are in some respects better off than welfare mothers in America. Nevertheless, 40 per cent of all female-headed families in Britain are below the poverty level.

The specific causes that distinguish female poverty from male poverty have been analyzed in a study, *Women and Children: Alone and in Poverty*, made in 1981 for the National Advisory Council on Economic Opportunity (since abolished by the Reagan administration) by Diana Pearce and Harriette McAdoo. The authors list all the possible personal and social sources of poverty, and point out that of these about half – such as lack of education, inadequate skills, poor health, low work commitment, racism, lack of job opportunities – can apply equally to men and women. The other half apply to women only.

> Men generally do not become poor because of divorce, sex-role socialization, sexism or, of course, pregnancy. Indeed, some may lift themselves out of poverty by the same means that plunge women into it: The same divorce that frees a man from the financial burdens of a family may result in poverty for his ex-wife and children. (p. 17)

This distinct character of women's poverty has two sources: women bear the major responsibility for childrearing; and women's income and economic mobility are limited further by occupational segregation, sex discrimination and sexual harassment. The two are, of course, closely related.

The expectations placed on women from the time they are born direct their educational and job choices, and prepare them to accommodate all other interests to their family responsibilities, which are duly placed upon their waiting shoulders. Yet when they carry out these duties to the letter they are penalized.

There are, for example, 5.4 million 'displaced home-makers' in the US, women who never held a job but devoted themselves to their families, then overnight found themselves the sole support of their children when they lost their husbands through death, divorce or desertion. 'We're told that we'll marry and live happily ever after,' one of them told the *Boston Globe* (29 September 1982). Maureen Ekblom of Worcester, Massachusetts, mother of three, married right out of school and with no training or experience, said, 'It's a fantasy, but you believe it. Nobody gets married thinking they'll be divorced.'

Few of these women find training and appropriate jobs. When women go on welfare, however, they are declared a budgetary burden and, if they are unmarried mothers, are suspected of having had children in order to cadge federal funds. Yet the day care and job training that would help to make them self-sufficient is not available. At the same time, they may be required to work at low-paid public jobs in order to qualify for relief benefits.

If they try to get off welfare they are again disadvantaged. Sheila Kamerman (1982) has pointed out the built-in disincentives to work in the welfare program. If she takes a job, the welfare mother faces a cut in benefits equal to every dollar earned, as well as loss of entitlement to free medical care and reductions in child-care expense credits and in food stamps.

The poverty trap works the same way in Britain. The National Council for One Parent Families reports (1981, p. 2):

> In July 1981, a working single mother with two children aged 4 and 6 and earning £50 a week would have had a net weekly spending power of £50.90 after tax and taking account of all relevant benefits. A pay increase of £24 would leave her *worse off* by £13.96 a week as she would have to pay extra tax and would become ineligible for some benefits.

Her income, by the way, would be well below the average disposable income of a one-parent family, which in 1979 was £70.46, compared to £123.30 for a two-parent family.

The cure for male poverty is a job. A job may not be easy to find, but a man has a better chance of collecting severance pay and unemployment benefits than a woman, whose employment is more likely to be part-time, short-term, and non-unionized. A man does not have to refuse a job because of the hours or the travel time or because it involves being away from home or moving to another city. He is not asked to give up his job to care for a child or other relative. And if he is on welfare he won't have his benefits cut for 'cohabiting.'

The converse is true for women, but it doesn't stop there. Sawhill (1980) has shown that many welfare mothers would not benefit from taking a job because 'most occupations in the sector reserved for women do not pay enough to permit a family to subsist beyond the poverty line' (p. 209).

In one study she compared the earnings of female

employed heads of families with male heads to calculate the earning potential of welfare mothers. When the 'female' earning function was applied to non-working welfare mothers, Sawhill found that half of them would not be able to earn as much as they were receiving from AFDC. When, however, they were attributed the same earning potential as a man of the same age, race, education, family background and other characteristics, she concluded that only 17 per cent would be better off staying on welfare. The 'crowding of women into a relatively small number of low-paid occupations is a major reason for the poverty of female-headed families,' she noted (p. 209).

This crowding of women also accounts for the fact that while black women suffer severe environmental and educational handicaps in comparison to white women, the earnings of the two are much closer together than those of black and white men. This is not because black women are moving up, but because employers tend to treat all women the same – as secondary workers. All the differences between black and white women's earnings can be accounted for by education and region; in contrast, direct race discrimination by employers plays a large part in the male wage differential (Almquist, 1979). Thus the median annual income for gainfully employed white women in 1981 was $5,500, that for black $4,900, while the figures were $14,300 and $8,500 for white and black men respectively. The poverty-line income for a two-member family in that year was $5,900.

Michelene Malson (1982), reporting on the special position black women have held in the US labor force, notes, moreover, that the experience of black women often forecasts the coming experience of white women: high female labor force participation, dual-earner and single-parent families, once distinctive for the black population, are now typical for the nation. The high rate of poverty characteristic for black women may be looked on as an ominous prediction.

This pattern of occupational segregation applies with amazing uniformity to all the countries of the industrialized world, from Israel to the Soviet Union. If it produces a disproportionately large population of poor women in Britain and the US there is good reason to believe that it creates a similar low-income female population elsewhere, even in socialist countries that do not admit to having poverty. Newland (1981), for example, deduces economic disadvantage in a growing number of households headed by women alone in the Soviet Union from a sharply rising infant mortality rate, which suggests poor health in expectant mothers. Ivan Volgyes (1980) uses official statistics to document Hungarian women's poverty. He observes that in 20 per cent of Hungarian families the woman's earnings are the main or only income. Yet 53 per cent of women earn less than sufficient to maintain two people at the official subsistence level compared to 14 per cent of men.

More than half of employed women in Britain work in the distributive trades, in offices, as teachers or nurses, or in services like catering and cleaning. One-quarter work in manufacturing, and of these half are in the food, clothing, textile, footwear and electrical engineering industries. There is no such concentration in male employment. In 1977 only 13 per cent of employed women were skilled manual workers or held professional or managerial positions (Oakley, 1981).

According to a cross-national survey, the segregation of the job market in the twenty-four most industrialized Western countries that belong to the Organization for Economic Cooperation and Development shows a 'remarkably similar' pattern everywhere. Women are concentrated in clerical and service occupations, men in production and transport (*OECD Observer*, May 1980).

A six-nation survey of the private sector conducted in the early 1970s in France, West Germany, the Netherlands, Belgium, Luxembourg and Italy found most women employed in low-level jobs in small enterprises. Two-thirds or more were in women's ghettos in factories, offices or shops. Usually no man was discovered doing comparable work (Merkl, 1976).

In countries where the commitment to equality between men and women has been held up as an example, notably Israel and the Soviet Union, the principle has eroded over time. According to Rae Lesser Blumberg (1976), the kibbutzim, which were originally envisioned as agrarian socialist societies, have developed within a single generation

– between 1920 and 1950 – 'an extremely sex differentiated division of labor' (p. 321). As the kibbutzim industrialized, men became producers, women workers in the services. Today, she writes, less than 10 per cent of women remain in the sought-after agricultural jobs; the rest are in the laundry, the kitchen, and other service occupations. Moreover, the division of labor is now justified by 'innate sexual differences.' In Israel as a whole women's average hourly wages are 20 per cent lower than men's (McCrae, 1983).

For the Soviet Union, Lapidus (1978) and McAuley (1981) have shown that although female employment rates are exceptionally high, with almost all able-bodied women of working age in the workforce, the occupational distribution by gender is in many respects similar to that found in Western countries. Women are over-represented in traditional industries and especially in low-level white-collar work and the services. Where whole professions have become feminized, as teaching and medicine, they have lost status, and the pay compares unfavorably with that of a skilled worker.

Other countries, specifically Sweden and the German Democratic Republic, whose equality efforts are more recent but whose concrete legislative and policy steps are well in advance of the rest of the world, and which are among the record holders as far as percentage of women in paid employment is concerned, are unable to point to a decisive improvement in their labor market patterns.

When in 1968 the Swedish government announced the goal of sex-role equality it declared that not just women's position but men's too would be altered. Occupational segregation was first among the barriers between the sexes that were to come tumbling down. Yet fifteen years and much legislative activity later, with a record 75 per cent of women between 16 and 64 in the workforce, Sweden has one of the most segregated labor forces in Europe. Eighty per cent of women work in thirty job categories. Women hold only 16 per cent of blue-collar jobs, but they are 90 per cent of health workers, 80 per cent of clerical workers, and 76 per cent of workers in the services (H. Scott, 1982b). This is almost identical with the distribution in the US, where 80 per cent of women work in twenty-five job categories (Sokoloff, 1980).

An illuminating comparison of women's position in East and West Germany has been made by Harry G. Shaffer (1981), particularly significant because it involves two states sharing a single history and cultural background which, since World War II, have followed different socio-economic paths, one state socialist, the other free market. In the strongly pro-equality German Democratic Republic women have educational and training opportunities far in advance of those offered in the neighboring Federal Republic. Moreover, the GDR holds the world record in the availability of day care, providing accommodation for 60 per cent of children under 3 and 90 per cent of those between 3 and 6.

Shaffer nevertheless found that in both Germanies women were grossly under-represented in manufacturing (except in the conventionally female industries), in transportation and communications, and even more so in construction. They were heavily over-represented in the service industries, commerce and trade. This was also true of the distribution of females in training for skilled jobs. The concentration of women learning to be office workers, sales personnel, hairdressers and textile workers in the GDR approaches 100 per cent saturation.

This is particularly interesting since German Democratic women appear to have all the chips on their side. The industrial workforce has been expanding relative to the services, while this has not been true in Western Europe for two decades. Moreover, between 1955 and 1975 the male workforce actually declined by 325,000 while the number of women in paid work grew by more than half a million. This should have created an overwhelming demand for women in traditionally male occupations. Yet women flooded into the services, actually releasing men for industry (H. Scott, 1982c).

As women work in the same kinds of jobs all over the industrialized world we can anticipate that they will earn the same kind of wages, and indeed we will not be disappointed. Efforts to obtain equal pay for equal work date back almost one hundred years, yet legislation providing for the implementation of equal pay was not passed in most Western countries until the 1970s and it has proved inadequate and hard to enforce.

In Britain the Equal Opportunities Commission announced in its *Sixth Annual Report* that in 1981 'the extent to which individual women and men see the Equal Pay Act as providing a remedy worth seeking had reached an all-time low' (p. 1). Women's earnings relative to men's had 'settled in the range of 73–75%' and the Commission expected no further improvement unless the law was amended.

The European Court of the ten Common Market countries has found Britain in violation of the EEC Equal Pay directive. The present national policy is to reduce pay as the best way of encouraging employment. Since there is no universally applicable minimum wage in Britain, it is possible to cut wage rates by fragmenting work into part-time jobs and by privatizing jobs in the public sector; both techniques affect women more than men. At present 10 per cent of men and 23 per cent of women earn below the 'decency' threshold defined by the EEC.

Through consistent efforts by the trade unions to raise the pay rates for the lowest categories of workers the average hourly industrial wage of women in Sweden has risen to 90 per cent of men's. In white-collar employment, however, women's salaries average only 70 per cent of what men are paid. In the OECD countries, women's pay for *full-time, year-round* work ranges from an average of 57 per cent of men's in the US to 81 per cent in Sweden. It is 77 per cent in the Netherlands, 74 per cent in Austria, 73 per cent in France, 66 per cent in Canada, and 65 per cent in the UK (Janjic, 1983).

These differences in wage rates are largely accounted for by the concentration of women in poorly paid occupations. They do not reflect the level of actual earnings, since they do not take into account overtime, predominantly male, or the fact that a substantial proportion of women in many countries work part-time: in Sweden a record 45 per cent, in the UK 43 per cent, in Australia and East Germany 35 per cent, in West Germany and the US about 28 per cent. These are the jobs with the poorest prospects and the fewest benefits.

Thus in both the US and Sweden women's median

annual earnings are less than half of men's. Of Swedish women Birgitta Wistrand (1981) writes: 'Despite the fact that today more and more women work, fewer and fewer are able to support themselves, due to part-time work and lower pay' (p. 101). In Britain, when overtime was included, 54 per cent of employed women were classified as 'low-paid' in 1980, that is, at the level of eligibility for Supplementary Benefits, compared to 13 per cent of men (Glucklich and Snell, 1981).

Women are also the hardest hit by unemployment, and this is true even with the present pattern of lay-offs in traditional male industries like steel, autos and engineering. During the world recession in the mid-1970s, women were reported to be 60 per cent of the unemployed in Italy although less than one-quarter of the workforce. In Sweden, Belgium, France, West Germany, Austria and the US over half the unemployed were women (Newland, 1979). Swedish female unemployment rates averaged 35 per cent higher than male for the entire period of 1963–81. There was only one year (1968) when the women's rate was lower than that for men (Leighton and Gustafsson, n.d., p. 12). Official unemployment in the UK between 1974 and 1978 increased three times as fast for women as for men (Bird, 1980). As the figure for those out of work in the Western industrial nations approached 32 million, the *OECD Observer* reported that 'those people hardest hit are those whose supply has expanded most rapidly – youth and women. . . . In almost all countries the employment rate of women is higher than men' (March 1982, p. 9).

Giles Merritt in *World Out of Work* (1982) agrees that joblessness hits women harder than men, and adds that 'registered unemployment figures are not only misleading but irrelevant' (p. 41). He quotes Peter Drucker of the *Wall Street Journal* on official US figures: 'an Alice in Wonderland stew of apples, oranges and red herrings' (p. 43).

Merritt considers that 'discouraged workers' who have ceased registering as unemployed, plus those who were too discouraged to even bother to register, account for another 20 per cent at least in the UK. This seems like a conservative estimate. The trade-union-financed journal *Labour Research*, in its December 1982 issue, put the level of women's unemployment in the UK at *double* the government figure, and the total for men at 50 per cent higher than the official estimate.

Everywhere youth unemployment figures are double or triple those for adults, and young women are reported particularly likely to give up the search. The more intense the pressure the more inclined people are to drop out of the labor market, feeling that the effort is futile. The most likely to drop out are those who are made to feel they have the least claim to be there in the first place and the least to offer in the way of qualifications.

High unemployment, it has been argued on both sides of the Atlantic, is unfortunately necessary to bring down inflation. In fact, some sponsors of the theory hold, unemployment is not really all that high if you discount a lot of people on the labor force rolls who don't belong there. As President Reagan said at a luncheon with journalists in April 1982, reported in *Time* (12 July 1982), part of the reason for unemployment 'is not so much recession as it is the great increase in the people going into the job market, and ladies, I'm not picking on anyone, but [it is] because of the increase in women who are working today and two-worker families.'

The idea that it is not normal for women to work outside the home is still deeply ingrained in some supposed liberals. Marvin Harris, a widely read anthropologist, in his 'angry outcry' *America Now* (1981) finds a connection between crime in the streets, which he attributes to high black unemployment, and the influx of women into the labor market. Certainly, he emphasizes, he does not hold women 'responsible for changes in the economy that put blacks at a disadvantage,' or for the high inflation that converted the 'reserve army of white housewives' into paid workers. None the less it is his explicit message that 'if these women had stayed home,' society would have been forced to create conditions for the employment of black males in the traditionally low-paid female dead-end jobs. But of course they didn't.

Unwittingly therefore, white women, responding to their own economic imperative clothed in the rhetoric of sexual

liberation, are steadily tightening the vise that holds the
ghetto in its jaws. (p. 138)

Read Harris's rhetoric as you will, this says (among other
things that the reader may want to question) that women
have less right to a job than men. Another version of the old
chestnut about women who do not really need to work taking
jobs from those who do. It is hard to object because Harris
makes it racist to do so.

Many other politicians and academics have questioned
women's right to be workers with the same standing as men,
with less rhetoric perhaps, but with an effect on policy. Pat
Armstrong (n.d.) writes of Canada:

The government is dealing with the dramatically rising
unemployment rates by defining female unemployment
out of existence, by blaming women for the increase in
unemployment and unemployment insurance costs, by
cutting back in those areas where women are employed,
and by withdrawing funds from programmes designed to
help jobless women. (p. 2)

There are those who argue patience. With time, perhaps
slowly but still surely, they say, women will penetrate men's
occupations as they are beginning to do in the professions.
They see women gradually becoming accepted in non-tradi-
tional jobs and overcoming their lack of skills.

This optimism is based on a misreading of the evidence.
It is fostered by the tremendous play given in the media to the
two-career family, as though these successful families in
which both partners hold professional or managerial jobs
represented a cultural standard against which most working
couples could measure themselves.

Harold Benenson (1984) has undertaken to dissect the
myth of the dual-career family in the US, where it is most
consistently invested with the trappings of reality. He points
out, to begin with, that married women in the eight elite
professions (architect, college teacher, computer systems
analyst, doctor, engineer, lawyer, mathematician, scientist)
represented less than 1 per cent of all employed wives in
1979. Only 'tiny numbers of women' reach upper levels of

management. Moreover, far from being models of equality, these families reproduce traditional inequalities. At this level the earnings gap between women and their husbands, and between women and their counterpart men is greater than in more typical two-income families.

> The women who seek careers are first, among those least likely to marry or have children; second, if single and supporting families, will have family incomes 64–77 percent (or less) than those of married career men; third, if married, are more likely to divorce; and fourth, when they divorce, are certain to suffer precipitous decline (of possibly 30 to 60 percent or more) in family income. (p. 29)

One does not need a crystal ball to predict that in the coming decades the segregation of the labor market by gender will continue, with women, minorities (including women of course) and youth (including women) representing a permanent pool of the unskilled and semiskilled. The economists have already collected the facts.

Braverman (1974) points out that, in the US, industry has been declining in terms of the percentage of employment it represents in every classification since the 1950s. The stagnation of typically male industrial occupations and the expansion of service jobs has widened the wage gap between men and women because the industrial sectors pay wages that are above average, while the pay is below average in the areas where women are finding employment. By 1959 average wage rates in industry were 17 per cent higher than in the services and the gap has been increasing since. This growing divide, and the fact that 'the levels of pay in the low-wage industries and occupations are below the subsistence level' (p. 395) explain, as Braverman says, why in the 1960s poverty was discovered in the midst of plenty. It is also part of the answer to why so many families headed by women who work will continue to be poor.

In the face of shrinking demand, women will have an increasingly hard time finding jobs in industry outside of female ghettos, and there too opportunities are shrinking. US women are feeling the pressure to get out of well-paid, hard-hat construction jobs where, thanks to federal

affirmative action regulations, they had made some slight
headway in the 1970s. 'The ranks of construction trades-
women shrank 24% last year . . . while the industry's total
blue collar employment dropped just 4%,' reports the *Wall
Street Journal* (15 April 1982). Women have suffered directly
from the decline in many labor-intensive light industries
(textiles, clothing, toys, leather goods, microelectric
assembly) and the export of production to cheap labor areas
in Third World countries. In the Common Market countries
as a whole employment in textiles dropped by about one-third
between 1960 and 1977, a loss of 900,000 jobs (Janjic, 1983);
in the UK women's employment declined in all manufacturing branches during the 1970s.

Yet the process has only begun. Professor Eli Ginsberg of
Columbia University predicts that by 1995 only 15 per cent of
all US jobs will be in manufacturing. Merritt (1982), an
expert on the Common Market for the hard-headed London
Financial Times, presents an apocalyptic vision of half of the
100 million jobs in manufacturing in the wealthy West
exposed to extinction due to the introduction of automation,
biological processes in industry, and the decline of traditional
fields.

The second major reason that job segregation will
increase and opportunities for women diminish is the introduction of the microchip into office work, which is overwhelmingly female. We do not yet have a clear picture of
what the full effect will be, but devastating is the word that
comes to mind. Even before the advent of the chip clerical
work, originally thought of as a good cut above the shop floor
in status, was losing its attraction and its prestige as a result
of mechanization. Today office workers represent some kind
of a new proletariat, with wages far lower than those in
industry and few of the fringe benefits. While work in a
mechanized office is routine it still involves the human brain.
Most work in a computerized office requires no skill that
cannot be learned in a short time, the jobs are monotonous
and the strain is almost unbearable (Braverman, 1974).

Referring to the worldwide impact of the new forms of
office technology, Warskett (1981) cites numerous studies
that put the potential reduction in clerical employment at

one-half or more. Moreover, 'the traditionally lower training levels and mobility of women may exaggerate the problem by restricting the number of computer-related occupations open to them' (Varette and Warskett, 1981, p. 17).

Many clerical jobs have already been lost and many more job losses are ahead, according to a study made for the Commission of the European Communities (Common Market countries) at the University of Sussex by Christine Shannon and Felicity Henwood (1982). The new jobs – fewer in number – created by information technology are chiefly in data processing, programming and systems analysis. These, the authors point out, are not areas in which large numbers of women are employed, and women are likely to find transition to these jobs more difficult than men because:

the jobs require a high level of technical skill, which
    women are less likely to have;
men regard these jobs as 'theirs,' and have already showed
    themselves unwilling to relinquish control over them;
women are less likely than men to have access to
    retraining within firms and industries;
women's lack of involvement at all levels of union
    organization makes them powerless in the face of
    discrimination.

Emma Bird (1980), in a study made for the British Equal Opportunities Commission, holds that the 'protection' against unemployment that women 'enjoyed' as a result of their willingness to work for low pay is evaporating, since it is just those low-level, repetitive jobs that can be computerized. Over a three-year period at American Telephone & Telegraph 22,000 women lost jobs because of automation, while 13,000 new positions were obtained by men (Hacker, 1981). Women's jobs will disappear in non-clerical fields too, since new versions of electromechanical products can be assembled, checked and sorted by video systems.

The effect of these two trends – the withering away of the mass industries and the computerization of white-collar employment – can hardly be overestimated. Merritt (1982) sees the loss of office jobs as the first stage, followed by a massive decline in blue-collar employment, affecting

anywhere between one-third and two-thirds of all jobs by the
end of the century. He finds polarization already taking
place, with the highly skilled at one end and the unskilled at
the other together making up a larger percentage of the
workforce.

We can anticipate that displaced skilled craftsmen and
young men who in the past would have trained for highly
paid manual jobs in traditional industries will present
unequal competition for women. They will take over not only
the skilled jobs and posts offered by the new technology in
whatever 'growth industries' eventually emerge, but the jobs
requiring high-level skills in office work, banking and
insurance. Women's jobs will require fewer skills.

Predictions may differ, but there is no doubt in anyone's
mind that a technological revolution of vast implications is
taking place that will affect men's and women's work and
their control over their lives in as yet unforeseen ways.
Women are far less well equipped than men to meet the new
situations.

Feminists have pointed out that women do have an
option. As Jan Zimmerman (1981) puts it, 'Women can park
themselves in the path of technological determinism.' They
can educate themselves in science and mathematics and
demand a voice in the development and application of technology (p. 365). In theory this is possible. In practice time is
running out and not much is happening.

Although women's general educational level has
advanced tremendously in the industrialized countries in
recent decades, education for women is not the key to the
distribution of life's chances that it is for men. In the US, a
woman with a university degree will earn less in her lifetime
than a man who does not finish secondary school. Most UK
schools exert pressure on girls to make conventional choices
and to accept the world as male outside the domestic sphere
(Mahony, 1982; Spender, 1982; Stanworth, 1983). Women do
not learn marketable skills, or at best they study nursing or
typing (Newland, 1979, 1981). Pearce and McAdoo (1981) cite
a study made in the US in the 1970s to locate ten secondary
schools that were 'pacesetters' in channeling girls into non-
traditional occupations. None were found. Even in Eastern

Europe, where women are encouraged to acquire skills, they end up overwhelmingly studying typically female occupations (Lapidus, 1978, 1980; McAuley, 1981; H. Scott, 1974; Shaffer, 1981; Volgyes, 1980).

Women who do make unconventional choices do not get jobs in their chosen field as easily or get ahead as fast as their male counterparts. They meet discouragement and often open hostility from management, male workers and unions.

Women are thus trapped in an endless circle. The unhappy prospect is for a further deterioration of their position with respect to men and of their chances of staying out of poverty.

Chapter 3

THE POOREST OF THE POOR

Seventy-five per cent of the world's population live in developing countries where the per capita income is less than $1000 a year. Of the 3.5 billion people who inhabit the vast continents of Asia, Africa and Latin America, three out of four live in the countryside. The majority of Third World women make their homes in these crisis areas; for East and West Africa and much of Asia the figure is over 80 per cent.

In the face of such pervasive distress, what is the justification for starting a discussion of poverty with the relatively luxurious penury of the developed world? Simply that the model of development being offered Third World women is the same one that has put us where we are. Having gained an idea of which way we are headed, we may find it easier to understand what is happening to women in countries most of us know only from reading the newspaper.

Like the poverty in our own countries, that in the Third World had to be 'discovered' anew after World War II. Even today its actual extent can only be estimated. Sivard (1982) has put the number of people throughout the world who live in 'extreme' poverty – that is, lack the most basic necessities – as high as 1000 million, most of them in the Third World. The Food and Agriculture Organization of the UN calculates those suffering from severe protein malnutrition at 500 million (Harrington, 1977, p. 60). According to an *OECD Review* estimate in 1977, 700 million were existing in 'absolute poverty,' with additional millions just above marginal subsistence (Galbraith, 1979, p. 43), while Lucille Mair of the UN Children's Fund has said that 'absolute poverty' applies to more than 500 million people in Asia alone (*Harvard Gazette*, 17 April 1981).

What does Asian 'absolute poverty' look like? In tiny Bangladesh with a population of 90 million, the per capita income is $90 a year, but in fact for the rural 90 per cent it is much less. Forty per cent of families are destitute and landless; 60 per cent suffer malnutrition. Millions have jobs that pay nothing; they work for food alone. One out of four children dies before the age of 5. The story is not very different in Sri Lanka, Indonesia, Pakistan, Malaysia and parts of India.

More appalling than figures like these, whose very size makes them hard to absorb, is the fact that the gulf separating rich and poor is increasing, nationally and internationally. Between 1952 and 1972 the gap between the per capita incomes of the poor and rich countries doubled (Harrington, 1977). While the per capita income of the poorest fifth of the world grew an average of $54 annually between 1960 and 1980, the annual per capita income of the richest fifth was augmented by an average of $4,224.

At the same time, within the poor countries themselves the spread between the poor and the rich has expanded. It is not unusual, writes Sivard (1982) for the richest fifth of a country to receive 60 per cent or more of the national income, while 2–5 per cent falls to the poorest fifth. There are extreme examples like Mexico, where two-thirds of the national income goes to 1 per cent of the population (Elmendorf, 1976).

A decline or stagnation in wages, income and consumption has been documented for the rural population throughout the Third World. This is not because there has been no increase in production. In fact, food output and growth in GNP have both outstripped population growth.

> In the Third World as a whole the rate of growth in the last quarter century or so has been unprecedented. Never before have so many poor countries – containing such a large proportion of those who are inadequately fed, clothed and housed – enjoyed such a period of rapid and sustained expansion of output. Yet . . . the problems of widespread poverty seem to have remained as great as ever. (Griffin, 1978, p. 145)

After a quarter of a century of orthodox insistence that

unrestricted international exchange would bring benefits to all, the reason poverty – and with it hunger, illiteracy, unemployment and excessive population growth – had proved intractable was located by many economists in the development model pressed on the Third World by the First. This model of economic expansion, whose benefits were expected to 'trickle down' to those at the bottom, embodied the same idea of progress as that which was supposed to have cured poverty in the industrial West. This assumes that technological development and modernization eventually help everyone.

Recalling the design of strategies to aid developing countries in the US after World War II, economist John Kenneth Galbraith (1979), former US Ambassador to India, argues that the cause of poverty was defined to fit the remedy available, rather than the treatment chosen to fit the disease. The cause of poverty could not be found in the inequities of the capitalist system, because that would have been unacceptable reasoning for Western governments and agencies.

> What was available in abundance was technology and capital, so the cause of poverty became technical backwardness and lack of capital. . . . But diagnosis which proceeds from the available remedy cannot be successful. (p. 42)

Mahbub ul Haq (1976), who served as Minister of Planning in the Pakistan Government and is now a World Bank Official, traces the rise and fall of the 'growth' ideology. Remembering his optimistic days as an economic planner for his country in the 1960s, he writes: 'We were confidently told that if you take care of your GNP, poverty will take care of itself' (p. 32). This strategy was

> based on the quiet assumption that poverty can be taken care of through high growth rates, which will eventually filter down to the masses. In this strategy, high growth rates are always better than low growth rates and distribution can be taken care of after growth is achieved. Both these premises have proved bankrupt by now. . . . If society has increased its income in the form of luxury

housing and motor cars, how do you really convert it into
low-cost housing and public buses, short of their physical
take-over by the poor? (pp. 41–2)

Third World poverty, like First World poverty, was
found to be a function of inequality, and the tendency of the
system was to multiply inequality as it went along. Opportunities benefited those who already had them. Capital
generated profits that found their way back to the First
World where interest rates on investments were higher,
instead of being invested in schools, health and clean water.
Local elites skewed development toward export agriculture,
heavy industry and urban growth. Technology and new agricultural techniques helped local entrepreneurs who had
started out with sufficient land or money to make use of them,
displacing poor farmers who became agricultural laborers or
migrated to the cities.

Objections by Third World governments to the im-
balances being created by the economic relations between the
industrialized West and their own countries reached a climax
in 1975 at the Seventh Special Assembly Session of the UN
General Assembly in 1975. In 1976, at the meeting of the UN
Conference on Trade and Development, the demand was
again put forward for a New International Economic Order
that would improve the conditions of trade and of the transfer
of investments and technology, as well as international
monetary reforms to stop the flow of money out of the Third
World and raise the share of these countries in industrial
production and food output. A program of action adopted by
the UN General Assembly has the long-term aim of reducing
Third World dependence on the industrialized countries.

So far in this chapter women have hardly been mentioned. This is because, during this quarter of a century of
controversy about the extent and cause of poverty and its
treatment, the missing actors on the international stage
were those who carry the main burden of rural poverty. It was
taken as given by First and Third World economic planners,
economists, businessmen and politicians that poverty was
the poverty of male farmers and male wage earners and male
unemployed, and that their wives were fully occupied at

home taking care of the children and perhaps a few domestic animals. Women entered the picture as ignorant breeders of large families at whose door much of the responsibility for Third World poverty could be laid. *UN Development Issue Paper* no. 12 (issued by the UN Development Programme in 1980, long after the fact) reports:

> There is only one reference to women in the resolution adopted by the UN General Assembly at its September 1975 Seventh Special Session on Development and International Economic Co-operation. It concerns the female biological role. 'Maternal and child health and family welfare' are to be included in community primary health services. (p. 1)

As it had been assumed that the Third World would automatically gain from economic development that benefited the First World, so it was taken for granted that women would be assisted by measures designed to improve the terms of development for Third World men. It never occurred to the proponents of growth or to the dissenters who pressed for a New International Economic Order that the strategies they were devising to help visible men might undermine the economic position of women – and in the long run defeat any recovery program. They either did not know or did not want to know about women's role in development.

We would not know about it either, were it not for the explicitly woman-oriented research undertaken in the past decade by Third and First World women, research whose impetus was provided by the women's liberation movement, even though all those engaged in this work would not describe themselves as feminists. These studies now fill numerous annotated bibliographies each almost as long as this book (see, for example, Buvinic, 1976; Cebotarev *et al.*, 1982; Vavrus and Cadieux, 1980). Calls for the inclusion of women in development began in the early 1960s as a result of seminars, often international in character, that were held on the status of women in a number of Third World countries. In 1970 Esther Boserup, a Danish economist, published her now-classic *Women in Development*, which literally revolutionized thinking about the role of women in Third World economies and what was happening to them as a result of 'modernization' by indigenous and foreign capitalism.

Again, these findings might have gathered dust on the shelves of academic institutions and foreign agencies, along with other occasional studies on the status of women, if it had not been for the UN decision to mark the mid-point of its Development Decade in 1975 with an International Women's Year and a conference on the position of women in Mexico City, which would in turn launch a UN Decade for Women.

The demand for an international women's year originated with the women's movement in the US, the UK and West Germany, where women wanted to see the issue of inequality on the UN agenda. To meet the objection of the Soviet Union and the other socialist countries, which claimed that they had already solved the problem of equality for women, and of Third World countries that development must come first, the UN Conference on the Position of Women was held in Mexico City in July 1975 with the triple theme of equality – development – peace (Stephenson, 1982). While this was attended by delegations appointed by governments, a parallel forum held by the non-governmental agencies affiliated with the UN attracted non-official women from all over the world.

These events, in spite of concerted media campaigns to obscure the issues and uncover headline-worthy feminist squabbles, heralded what has become a continuing worldwide debate, and has made research on women respectable and mention of women in international documents compulsory. What had emerged from Boserup's findings, and has been amply confirmed since, is that women are the major food producers everywhere in the Third World, accounting for as much as 60–80 per cent of output. Farming is not all they do. They carry home fuel and water, spin, weave, preserve food and sell their surplus. They cook and care for their children and very often for the elderly and disabled as well. The typical African woman's day has been put at fifteen or sixteen hours.

The impact of development, far from easing most women's work, has been to take from women what economic independence they had in their earlier tribal societies. The crucial issue, first raised by Boserup, is that economic development of the kind imported into Third World countries creates structural changes that force women from positions where they enjoyed some income and status, and at the same time adds additional hardships to their responsibilities as family providers.

The erosion of women's position began under colonial rule – the Spanish in Latin America, the British in India and the Caribbean, the French, Dutch and Germans in Africa. Europeans, says Boserup, had little sympathy for the female farming systems they found in their colonies. The land tenure rights which women held in many tribal societies were simply taken away from them and the land was given to men. Inheritance laws were changed so that land was no longer handed down through the female line. As cash crop plantations growing coffee, sugar, cotton, tea or bananas crowded out farming for local markets, men were hired for the work in conformity with European nineteenth-century beliefs regarding the 'natural' division of labor. The Bible, following the Flag, explained that this was the way God wanted it.

While women were deprived of their land and relegated to subsistence farming, although agriculture was traditionally a female occupation, modern farming techniques were being taught to men. This enabled some of them to plant cash crops on their own holdings and to benefit from government farm services. The gap between male and female productivity and earnings widened. 'It is men who do the modern things . . . men ride the bicycle and drive the lorry, while women carry headloads . . .' (Boserup, 1970, p. 56).

Although the colonizers have left, their policies have remained. The industrial nations still control the capital, technology and markets. According to Boserup, in Asia and many places in Africa many of the plantations established in colonial times are still owned and run by Europeans. Further vast tracts of land are no longer planted to supply food to the population because they have been taken over by highly industrialized internationally owned farming enterprises producing for the export market. An article in the London *Guardian* of 14 January 1977 cited by Stuckey and Fay

(1980), puts the acreage dominated by multinational agri-business at three-quarters of the world's agricultural land. In Latin America, for example, the per capita production of subsistence crops decreased by 10 per cent between 1964 and 1974, while export production of agricultural products rose by 27 per cent (Arizpe and Aranda, 1981).

With the spread of agribusiness and the establishment of new industries, farming for food in Africa has become more and more a female occupation. Boserup reports that the sub-sistence farming system can operate normally in parts of Africa with 60–75 per cent of the male population absent. Michael Harrington (1977), a journalist more observant than most planners engaged in the transfer of technology, observed that in Kenya

> women do most of the farm work; they are about two-thirds of the rural population. The men tend the cattle, but that is usually all they do. Otherwise they engage in trade, work in the city and lead a social life that takes as much time as work itself. (p. 173)

The technical solutions that Western nations believed would enable former colonial countries to 'catch up' had, by the late 1960s, been shown to reproduce national and class divisions of labor in the process of transfer. They require capital, research, and organizational chains of command at the top and a large waged labor force at the bottom. More recently it has become obvious that there is also a gender bias in all our assumptions about technology, and these are also built into our technological aid to developing countries.

The new technology that might lighten women's in-creased work in food production rarely finds its way to them, because men are the ones who are acquainted with new machinery in development projects regardless of who normally performs the job to be mechanized. This is routine practice for Western technical advisors, themselves men (Anderson, 1983; D'Onofrio-Flores, 1982; Tinker, 1976). Kirsten Sorgensen, a Danish expert working at the Center for Development Research in Copenhagen, who was studying the impact of drinking water projects on African rural women, found nothing on the subject in the literature. Yet, as she pointed out, women and children should be the main targets of such programs since it is they who fetch the water and women who use it in cooking and washing. Nevertheless, pumps continue to be designed too heavy for women and children to operate, and children cannot reach the tap (Kneerim and Shur, n.d.).

In Africa women are engaged on cash crop plantations rarely. In Asia, where the agricultural system calls for the use of entire families, men are employed for wages while women are paid piece rates, requiring many more hours to produce subsistence earnings. Women are called upon to do the arduous unskilled work, weeding and gathering. In North India, Boserup (1970) reports, women work picking tea leaves:

> A woman's day begins at 4 or 5 a.m. with cooking for the family. Then, after seven or eight hours of plantation work, she must fetch water and firewood and cook another meal. Children are often brought to the fields, the small ones strapped to the back of the mother. (p. 78)

The conventional picture of Arab Muslim women at home behind the veil, supported by their male relatives, has also been modified. Strict seclusion is true only for middle-class families. The majority of women are peasants in rural areas, engaged in subsistence farming without pay and without veils. They participate in all types of farm work and often do more than the men (Minces, 1980; El Saadawi, 1982).

In Latin America as well, capitalist development appears to increase the participation of landless and small-holder women in work on subsistence plots and as wage laborers on large estates. In some cases their wages are close to half of what men are paid; in others the man is paid for the work of his wife and children (Tadesse, 1982).

This does not end the unfavorable effects of development on women. Market trade has been another traditional source of income for women in Africa and South East Asia, outside of Muslim areas, and in parts of Latin America as well. Now the development of a modern retail trade sector is crowding women out, since most shop assistants in the new stores are men. Similarly the cottage industries that were open to women even in Muslim countries have been giving way to foreign or domestically owned factories employing chiefly men.

Paid agricultural work is declining for many women and other opportunities are shrinking because agriculture is releasing people faster than they can be absorbed by industry. In India, where 90 per cent of the population is rural,

> development has exacted a terrible price from women. . . . Pesticides and harvesting machines have taken over their jobs of weeding, harvesting, planting and sowing. Despite increases in population, the number of women agricultural workers declined by half between 1961 and 1971 (the last census year), and farm jobs are the main paid work available to women. . . . Unorganized cottage industries like handicrafts, tanning, weaving, oil pressing and rice pounding have simply died because they couldn't compete with modern factories. What work remains on the farms and in household cottage industries has been taken over by the increasing number of unemployed men. (Chacko, 1980, p. 5)

Women who find their way to the cities on their own in the hope of bettering themselves, or who accompany their husbands when the family has been forced off the land, most frequently find work as domestic servants or in the 'informal sector,' the euphemism for the multitude of services, uncontrolled by labor laws, that supply the predominantly male labor force in the shantytowns surrounding Third World cities. Women's work may be an extension of their domestic roles, such as cooking, laundry and ironing, babysitting, gardening. They cook and sell food to workers on job sites, are street vendors, waitresses, entertainers or prostitutes. This kind of service work, typical for Latin America where nearly 60 per cent of the population now lives in urban centers, is exceptionally vulnerable to exploitation.

On the other hand, urban women in Latin America have access to some industrial employment and make up about 25 per cent of all workers in manufacturing, compared to only 9 per cent in Muslim North Africa (Youssef, 1977). In West

Africa most factories are closed to women. Women's share of employment in India's textile industry has declined to 6 per cent, compared to twice that in construction, where their tasks include carrying headloads of building materials. They are paid less than men, less than the minimum wage, less in fact than a woman needs to feed herself (Boserup, 1970; Caplan, 1979). 'Millions of women in dozens of other countries in Asia, Africa and Latin America face growing competition in crowded labor markets' (Newland, 1979, p. 144).

Ironically, the spread of modern capitalist production and technology in the Third World, rather than creating the stable male-headed family so ardently advocated by colonial missionaries, has produced woman-headed households in greater proportions than those reported in the industrial countries. This is true for Africa, where men migrate in search of factory jobs or are absorbed by agribusiness leaving women and children in the village, and of urban Latin America, where many women find they can do better by combining households with other female relatives than they can by living with a man. In Muslim Asia and North Africa the protection traditionally provided by male relatives to widowed or divorced women is breaking down for economic reasons, and such women are increasingly found in paid employment (Mernissi, 1976; Tinker, 1976; Youssef, 1977; Newland, 1979). According to a report in *Women at Work*, a publication of the International Labor Organization (1982, no. 1, p. 12):

> The reality in developing countries is that women increasingly are the *de facto* heads of households with full responsibility for their own and their children's survival. Households headed by women account for 35 per cent of households in many parts of the Caribbean and 42 per cent of households in Botswana. The proportion of such households is rising everywhere; between 1960 and 1970 it had doubled in Brazil and increased by one-third in Morocco. . . . Women headed households (with children) are significantly poorer than men's.

Lesotho, an independent state completely surrounded by

the Republic of South Africa, provides the most cynical commentary of them all on the dedication of capitalism to family values. Most of the male workforce of Lesotho is employed in South African mines, but Lesotho women are not allowed to reside in the Republic. They consequently live apart from their male relatives for a year or two at a time, during which time they are often without cash resources (Mueller, 1977).

There are jobs in manufacturing that have opened up for Third World women over the past two decades, jobs that link the fate of women in the capitalist West and the undeveloped South and East in a direct way. These opportunities are in 'world market factories' in free trade zones, established by agreement between the governments of industrialized countries and those of poor states – most of them in Asia and Latin America – hungry for transfusions of capital. To these free trade zones, areas designed for the exclusive use of foreign investors, come multinationals that are tired of paying trade union wages and social benefits and are looking for cheap labor.

They or their wholly or partly owned subsidiaries get that and a great deal more: removal of trade and currency restrictions, exemption from duties and taxes, preferential tariff rates and transport facilities, and other incentives. They also have the cooperation of the host governments, which see to the suspension or abrogation in these areas of such social legislation and trade union rights as had been won. The only requirement on the companies is that they export their goods.

Unlike the import substitution industries established earlier to produce for the local market, which employed men, these factories making labor-intensive light industry products (especially clothing and electronic components, but also toys, musical instruments, sporting goods, leatherware and optical products) seek out unmarried women between 18 and 24 years of age. Many of the First World women who used to make those pullovers now labelled 'Made in Hong Kong' and those stuffed toys marked 'Made in Korea' are now unemployed, the European textile and garment industry having laid off one million workers during the 1970s (Merritt, 1982). Their Asian, African and Latin American sisters work for one-tenth the wages or less, and none of the fringe benefits. Cheap enough to make it profitable for trousers cut out in Germany to be flown in air containers to Tunisia to be sewed and then flown back to Germany to be sold (Elson and Pearson, 1981). Levi Strauss, makers of blue jeans, alone employ 44,000 workers outside the US in twenty-four factories which provide 35 per cent of their profits.

The promotion of these special production areas where normal taxes and regulations do not apply, and assistance in their planning and in the construction of factories, has become one of the major activities of the UN Industrial Development Organization (UNIDO) in its effort to establish export-oriented industries in the developing countries. When a West German team of economists investigated the ramifications of this program in 1975 there were 750,000 people employed in twenty-seven of the thirty-nine countries where free production zones were in operation, while world factories with similar privileges existed outside the zones in another twelve countries (Fröbel *et al.*, 1980). It seems safe to estimate the present figure at easily double that number. Other investigations confirm the findings of the German authors that work in these zones is characterized by exceptionally low wages, long hours, speed-up, inadequate health care, disregard for workers' living conditions, strict discipline, and intimidation to keep the unions away (Elson and Pearson, 1981; Lim, 1981; Safa, 1981).

The free trade zone of Banyan Lepas, Penang, Malaysia was established in 1974 on land which had belonged to independent farmers whom the government had resettled in remote regions in the interior. It is now occupied exclusively by foreign electronics firms. When Anne-Marie Münster (n.d.) interviewed workers there in 1980 she found the daily wage to be one-tenth that paid in the industry in West Germany. While in Germany employers were paying their employees the equivalent of 65 per cent extra in the form of benefits (holidays, medical care, pensions, etc.), social expenditures paid out for Penang workers amounted to 10–20 per cent of wages.

Many of the women employed in world market factories live at home and travel long distances to work. Others stay in cheap boarding houses. Gillian McCredie, who visited the Bataan free trade zone in the Philippines for the London *Guardian* (*Manchester Guardian Weekly*, 28 March 1982) reported young women living five or six to a room. 'You have only body space,' she was told. Workers complained of being made to work continuous shifts through the night with the doors locked so that they could not leave.

Although one ostensible purpose of these factories was to help relieve unemployment in the Third World they have not had this effect, since employers prefer to hire very young women who have not worked before and will leave, to be replaced by others, when they get married, rather than take men from the rolls of the unemployed. Employers seek young women because of their 'nimble fingers' and their 'docility.' As a US businessman in Mexico told another *Guardian* reporter, Lindsey Hilsum:

There's no welfare here. You can punish Mexican workers. Also there's the 48-hour week. You don't see any horsing around here, no queues for the water-fountain or the bathroom. These girls work. (*Manchester Guardian Weekly*, 28 March 1982)

Men wouldn't do this kind of tedious work, it is said. 'It goes against a man's macho pride.'

The majority of the women workers in free trade zones contribute to the support of their parents, whether they live at home or near the factory. Often this is the family's only source of cash income. But what long-run benefits, if any, do the women derive from this kind of job? Very few, most observers think. One result in Mexico, for example, has been an increase in female-headed families. Turnover is high and women learn no real skills that they can use elsewhere. Typically, all cutters, pressers and those operating more complicated machinery are men. Many women turn to prostitution when they lose their jobs, particularly in areas patronized by Japanese tourists or US Army bases (Aguilar-San Juan, 1982). The harsh measures protecting the factories from labor unrest undermine the position of labor generally (Elson and Pearson, 1981; Safa, 1981).

As a result of research like that described in this chapter

it has become *de rigueur* to mention women in connection with development. The governments of the world *did* adopt a Plan of Action at the UN Conference on Women in Mexico City, and they *were* going to have to report on their progress at the Mid-Decade Conference on Women in Copenhagen in 1980. Funding for private and government programs to help poor rural women has been channeled through various agencies. Resolutions have been passed by the UN linking the World Plan of Action for women with the New International Economic Order for the Third World, also endorsed by the UN. But women experts from various regions of the Third World have expressed the fear that NIEO goals, tied as they are to making cash crops more productive, expanding agribusiness, enlarging technological and scientific capabilities of Third World countries and increasing their industrial potential, will not reverse the trend toward displacing women and using them as cheap labor.

Irene Tinker (1981), who was instrumental in organizing the Seminar on Women in Development held in connection with the first UN world conference of the Decade for Women in 1975, charges that the male establishment does not take women seriously. Commenting on the Mid-Decade Conference at Copenhagen in 1980, she writes that not the US State Department nor the UN Secretariat nor the governments of the less developed countries

> gives any standing in their priorities to women's issues. Hence, at the official conference there are no negotiating positions. No government or group really wants anything for women enough to compromise on other issues. . . . Once the debate moves to the New International Economic Order (NIEO), the issue is no longer 'women's special needs' but rather nationalistic demands and the desires of women as citizens. . . . [Women] seldom are given the opportunity to take part in the other fora where the NIEO is debated. Women ought to be allowed to participate in a continuous way in the important and aggravating debate on the New International Economic Order, not confined to a five-year cycle of appearances. (pp. 533–4)

If women's position is not changed fundamentally – and

the conditions for this do not at present exist – economic development will continue to increase women's poverty relative to men's even if the governments of the less developed countries succeed in improving their countries' position *vis-à-vis* the industrialized world. Women view the kind of development aid they are receiving with reservations. Third World women need cash income, and 'income-generation projects' have become fashionable with development agencies. Delegates representing Third World women's organizations, who attended workshops held during the non-governmental Forum that was held in Copenhagen in 1980 while the UN women's conference was in session, questioned the value of programs designed to set up small workshops or market home-made goods. These were characterized as survival tactics, measures that isolated women still further from the market and camouflaged unemployment.

Why should women move into handicrafts when men are moving out, they asked. Who is looking at the root causes of women's poverty? Who is doing anything about the infrastructure: water, transportation, food preservation, day care? Women need credit, local leadership, training, access to technology. Why educate women in the old stereotypes, put them into the old exploitive jobs?

Amelia Rokotuivuna of Fiji was one who expressed her uneasiness that such programs absolve policy makers from having to pay attention to women in big development projects: 'What I fear about the women's movement is that we'll wake up and all we'll have are income-generating projects, supported by the government – because they will keep the women happy and quiet' (Kneerim and Shur, n.d., p. 31).

Women have special problems of education and health that are still not being met. In Africa 88 per cent of women are illiterate compared to 66 per cent of men, and this 20-point gap is typical. Asian illiteracy rates for women range from 87 per cent in India to 52 per cent in Hong Kong. An illiterate woman cannot read the instructions for operating machinery or open a bank account (Kneerim and Shur, n.d.; Tinker, 1976). Accelerated introduction of education is increasing the literacy gap. In many countries the school system cannot expand as fast as the population is growing;

the majority of children who are sent to school in this situation are boys. Worldwide, the number of men who cannot read or write grew by 8 million between 1960 and 1970, but the number of women rose by 40 million (Newland, 1979).

Women's health is more at risk than men's in Third World countries. Boy children are fed better than girl children because they are more important to the family economy. They are also more likely to receive medical care. Women, who need extra nutrition during pregnancy and nursing, usually have a diet inferior to men's. Often they eat only what is left after the men finish. Access to maternal health and family planning services, where these exist, is limited not only by ignorance and the prejudice of husbands but by lack of time and transportation. Commercial infant formulas, widely promoted by multinationals as a substitute for breastfeeding, introduce a new threat to the health of babies when they are pressed on Third World mothers without regard for local conditions.

The charge that women's position in the less developed countries is deteriorating is not the result of random impressions. UN material distributed in preparation for the official Copenhagen conference on women, based on information supplied by eighty-six countries, showed that since 1975

in most countries the situation of women from the so-called 'backward sectors' of the population had worsened . . . in particular with respect to employment and education for women in rural areas and in the so-called marginal urban sectors. . . . Illiteracy rates had increased in most developing countries, educational gains made by middle and upper income groups had not been followed by increases in the levels of employment, and the inadequate application of technology had created adverse conditions for the employment of many women. (Quoted in Leacock, 1981b, pp. 474–5)

This same UN bulletin gave three major reasons for the failure of equal rights legislation to bring about substantial improvements of women's position in almost all the countries supplying information: attitudes of male supremacy, the 'invisibility' of women's unpaid labor, and the structure of the world economy. In the next chapter we will look at some of the ways in which these three interact.

Chapter 4

LABOR, PAID AND UNPAID

I was a professional until my marriage three years ago. We now have a 2-year-old, and I gave up my profession to be a full-time mother. My husband and I have been fighting about money ever since. . . . Can anyone offer me guidelines – what would be reasonable, what would be fair? Do other stay-at-home women feel frustrated by their lack of financial power?

Just so you know what my situation is, my husband earns in excess of $50,000 a year, and my 'allowance' is $15 a week. . . . Since we've been married I have bought no new clothes except for two pairs of shoes, and I have no other money myself. I hate to say it, but I think my husband is being cheap. What do you think? (from an advice column in the Boston *Globe*, 2 February 1983)

Most women among the 'visibly' poor have fallen below the poverty line because they never were or are no longer married. Here is one who has become poor – if invisibly so – just because she married. A former professional, she now can't buy a pair of blue jeans. Something is wrong, but she is not quite sure what.

The two sources of women's poverty – their unpaid labor in the family and their consignment to jobs in a female ghetto of poorly paid work – are closely related but the twisted strands of this relationship are difficult to follow. In 'common sense' explanations women's lower status on the job market is made to follow logically from a biologically determined destiny.

Women are mothers and therefore concern for the family comes 'naturally' before everything else; they are physically weaker than men; their skills, aptitudes and character attributes make them less likely to succeed; they do not have the same commitment to a job that men do; family responsibilities make them less reliable, and besides they don't need jobs as much as men do. Over the years these reasons have been shown up for what they are – rationalizations that make it possible to call discrimination by another name.

Woman's biological role in childbearing does not inevitably determine her social role. In all societies that we know of women do heavy work. They have showed themselves capable in all the jobs and professions traditionally considered male. But even when they are not tied down by children, have acquired the necessary training, are fired with ambition and can demonstrate the need to support themselves they do not have the same chance as men.

Mainstream economic theories of job segregation explain the consequences, not the cause. The 'human capital' theory argues that women do not invest the same time and money in fitting themselves for the labor market as men do. Other theories assume employer discrimination arising from women's 'less valuable' human capital and general unreliability. Women are then 'crowded' into female-typed occupation and this competition depresses wages (Strober, 1976).

It is becoming increasingly difficult to resist the idea that an artificial separation of life into two supposedly distinct spheres of activity, the 'public' and the 'private,' with women assigned to the second at the expense of their participation and influence in the first, is not a hangover from a less enlightened age but admirably serves to support male dominance in society at large and the profitability of our market economy. The enormous amount of unpaid work performed by women in the home and out of it is essential both to our patriarchal culture and to industrial capitalism. If it were not for the free ride these two mutually supportive, interlocking systems are receiving it would not have been necessary to disguise the economic value of women's work in the 'private' sphere with so much mythology.

The work women do 'in exchange for' food and lodging and sometimes pin money could not be purchased by any man, even one who could afford and find a full complement of services and servants. No one has calculated the advantage to men of the position of psychological and sexual dominance that the dichotomized family affords them, even in societies where women have won a long list of legal rights.

From the point of view of capital, try to imagine what it would mean if women laid down their tools. Women are on duty twenty-four hours a day; the emotional content of what they do gives their work its meaning for them. Reduced to sociological terms, they nurture the future labor force and keep the present one fit to report to work.

> The social division between the production sphere and 'private' life serves several functions, one of which is to leave the owners and decision makers in the sphere of production free to pursue their goals without great regard for the conditions of reproduction of labor. (Holter and Henriksen, 1979, p. 217)

If business had to replace all the merely material functions women perform with commercial services at rates the average working man could afford, or finance them in the public sector, its wages and tax bill would put the US budget deficit to shame. It would have to hire more people (presumably women) to provide these additional services. The whole project would require a shift in investments that would significantly alter the structure of the economy – perhaps for the better, but certainly not in line with the present concepts and priorities of male planners.

In spite of these quite obvious benefits to the economy, women are not perceived to 'work' in the home in the sense that men do on their jobs. Nothing a housewife does is of value in capitalist terms because it does not take place on the market and therefore does not contribute to the Gross National Product. Likewise in Marxist theory her activity, though 'useful,' is not 'productive' for a similar reason: the housewife does not sell her labor power on the market and therefore it is not a source of surplus value, of profit.

It follows, of course, that a housewife is not a member of the workforce, and when we look at the categories 'worker' or 'employee' or 'labor' we do not see her. Because of the generally accepted premise that unpaid work is not real work, housewives and other unpaid workers become invisible in an economic sense. Just as women drop out of sight when we apply to them conventional definitions of poverty and class, they slip through the statistics and disappear into catch-alls like family and household because we have no definition of work that holds them.

One of the contributions of the women's movement has been to raise (not for the first time in history) the question of the value of women's unpaid work (see, for example, the collection of articles on the 'domestic labor debate' in Malos, 1980). Although there is considerable difference of opinion over how the reality of this work should be treated in theory and practice, there is unanimity on its economic importance. Even the media usually take care now to distinguish women in paid work from full-time housewives instead of women who 'work' from those who 'don't.'

Economists too have noticed that something closely resembling work goes on in the household and results in products and services that closely resemble those commanding a price outside the home. For example, a US Social Security Administration estimate in 1981 put 'basic' home-making (not including all roles) at between $9200 and $12,600 annually (*The New York Times*, 4 April 1981). A publication of the International Labor Organization in Geneva reports that the value placed on production in the 'household sector' in various studies made in industrialized countries has been estimated at from 25 to 40 per cent of GNP. Its author, Luisella Goldschmidt-Clermont (1982), a Belgian economist, reviews some seventy-five of these evaluations, the majority made since 1960 in the US, Scandinavia, West Germany and France.

Different methods are used in imputing value in these investigations. Some researchers calculate the number of hours spent. Thus a French study put the time expended in housework in 1975 at 30 per cent more than that spent by the entire nation in paid work. Others use wage-based methods: what a domestic worker would be paid who performed all a housewife's tasks; or the average wages of labor market workers doing the same things; or wages foregone in the market by the woman who works at home. The Chase

National Bank, in a 1972 investigation entitled 'What is a wife worth?', using the hourly wage rates for nursemaid, dietician, housekeeper, chauffeur, and so on, concluded that an American housewife put in 99.6 hours weekly (double time was awarded for overlapping tasks like feeding the baby while cooking dinner) and valued her at $275.53 a week. If all unpaid housework had been paid at that rate it would have cost the country twice the national budget.

There are various methodological difficulties implicit in all the calculations that Goldschmidt-Clermont reviews, but she does not regard them as insurmountable obstacles to placing a monetary value on housework. She has since come up with a method of her own, based on the market price of household-produced goods and services (1983).

Are we now on the way to official recognition of house-work as having economic worth (i.e., of the fact that work is work), and logically to a totally new definition of the labor force that will include almost all women as it includes almost all men? Will the unions launch a new campaign for the eight-hour day?

Unfortunately it is not just a matter of the seriousness of the intentions of economic researchers. There are good reasons why cogent arguments have no more than a cosmetic effect. The advantage of the unpaid housewife to the employer is not only that she saves him part of the cost of reproducing the labor force. There is, for example, the fact that industry wants a motivated, mobile, highly productive workforce. Under the socially 'ideal' division of roles, the wife is expected to provide a supportive climate that makes it possible for her husband to devote all his attention, energy and competitive spirit to his job, an environment that renews him psychologically as well as physically.

This aspect of the complementary roles housewife/bread-winner is one that seriously concerns spokesmen for the New Right in the US, as Zillah Eisenstein (1982) has pointed out. Describing the argument of George Gilder in his *Wealth and Poverty*, one of President Reagan's favorite books, she writes: 'Disruption of family life creates disruption in the economy because men need to direct their sexual energies toward the economy, and they only do so when they are connected to family duty.' (p. 576) This, Gilder believes, is not true of women, who do not make earning money their top priority: 'Women's involvement in the labor force has challenged man's position of authority in the family, reduced his productivity at work, and thereby "caused a simultaneous expansion of the workforce and a decline in productivity growth." ' (p. 577)

These are two advantages that women's devotion to domestic work supplies for employers: the free day-to-day reproduction of the labor force and the maintenance of male supremacy in the home, which is supposed to contribute to his will as well as to his freedom to succeed on the job. A third and major advantage is that their unpaid work keeps down their wages when women do go out to work. This is usually explained by the 'cheap labor reserve' theory, and the argument is that because the support of wives is the responsibility of husbands women will work for less, and they can be called out of the home when needed and sent back when no longer necessary. This worked well during two world wars, when women workers were glorified for their ability to do 'a man's job' in the absence of men and then rapidly banished back to domesticity when peace was signed.

The flaw in the theory as far as explaining women's present deteriorating economic position is concerned is that women continue to function as cheap labor even when they are no longer a reserve. In the past twenty years they have become a large part of the permanent labor force. In the UK every second married woman of working age has a paid job. In 1979 in the US 59 per cent of women with children aged 6 to 17 and a husband present were in the workforce; 83 per cent of divorced women with children in that age group were gainfully employed. Swedish women hold a record; nearly 75 per cent of mothers of preschool children work outside the home.

The pattern of interrupting paid employment is . . . less pervasive than is generally thought. . . . In many countries the three-phase work-life of paid employment, unpaid child-rearing, and additional paid employment is becoming more the exception than the rule. (Newland, 1979, pp. 161–3)

Why does it work this way and why do women get the particular jobs they get throughout the industrialized world? Much is made of the fact that almost everything women do seems to be connected with personal services for others. Teaching, nursing, retail sales, the production of food and clothing, all seem closely joined to the services women supply for their families. We all know about the secretary who makes coffee, tidies the office, and reminds the boss of his wedding anniversary. The most important distinguishing feature of women's work, in the home and out, however, is that it is labor-intensive.

What work in a typing pool and on an electronic components assembly line have in common is not anything typically female. It is that these operations require a relatively large number of people. There are many other operations, especially in the services, that have proved difficult or expensive to mechanize. The same is true of caring for children, making beds, cleaning house, cooking for a small family. Since productivity is low, labor costs must be kept low. It is important that women continue to do the jobs in the home free because they are labor-intensive. Labor-intensive jobs are reserved for women outside the home just because women can be paid less. Braverman (1974) explains why the services are the new 'opportunities' for women:

It is characteristic of most of the jobs created in this 'service sector' that, by the nature of the labor process they incorporate, they are less susceptible to technological change than the processes of most goods-producing industries. Thus while labor tends to stagnate or shrink in the manufacturing sector, it piles up in these services and meets a renewal of the traditional forms of pre-monopoly competition among the many firms that proliferate in fields with lower capital-entry requirements. Largely nonunion and drawing on the pool of pauperized labor at the bottom of the working-class population, these industries create new low-wage sectors of the working class, more intensely exploited and oppressed than those in the mechanized fields of production.

This is the field of employment, along with clerical

work, into which women in large numbers are drawn out of the household. (p. 282)

When jobs can be mechanized or automated they are usually turned over to men. Agriculture provides us with a classic example; office work is about to provide us with another.

As long as work in the home is non-work, possessing no monetary value, it does not confer on a woman any claim to qualifications or work experience, although her training in the management of time and money, in dealing with people, in food purchasing, and so on, may be superior to that of some people in the paid workforce. An 'unskilled' housewife can only command an 'unskilled' job at low pay. The image of the housewife is that of a person who doesn't know how to do anything. The trade union will be the last to disabuse her of that idea.

This is, in the final analysis, why it is so necessary to maintain the myth that woman's place is in the home and that what she does there, while spiritually significant, is not real work. The system, as everyone knows who has experienced it, is self-perpetuating. The individual woman, with or without a family to care for, is the carrier of all those 'typically female' attributes which do not necessarily apply to her. They will determine her occupational entry point and future mobility. Her own choice, in so far as she is able to exercise it, will be influenced by the stereotypes she has made her own concerning what is suitable for a woman.

In its late-twentieth-century version, the ideology supporting the housewife/breadwinner division of labor makes it seem to be a necessary consequence of love. He 'supports' her and she serves him, as though their affection could not be expressed through any other arrangement. Boys and girls learn their lessons at their parents' knees; so in a few generations it seems as though it had never been otherwise. A young single mother recently recalled for me her brief married life:

> I became my mother the minute I said 'I do,' and I married a man just like my father. My mother thinks because the floor is clean she's beautiful. I used to spend every day cleaning. Then one day I couldn't any more. I just lay

around the house. He came home and started yelling. Like my father. I realized then how I had been role playing. That was the beginning of the end of my marriage.

Some economists argue that employers create unnecessarily complex hierarchical job stratifications and specializations in order to divide the labor force and enhance their control over it. They have noted in recent decades the emergence of two distinct labor markets with a relatively impermeable barrier between them. The first is characterized by highly structured jobs, good wages and conditions, regular employment and upward mobility; the other by poor conditions, lack of job security, and little opportunity for advancement.

Those who are hired for the 'primary' market, according to this 'dual labor market' theory, are considered to be stable and motivated; those who find their way into the 'secondary' market are seen to be unreliable, change jobs often and do not have a strong 'work ethic.' Workers who belong to a general category of people assumed to have undesirable characteristics are likely to be assigned jobs in the secondary labor market regardless of their personal qualities. The 'dual labor market' theory has been used to explain the concentration of minority and other disadvantaged workers in a labor market ghetto. This analysis also suggests a mechanism that helps keep women at the bottom (Gordon, 1972; Blau and Jusenius, 1980; Sokoloff, 1980).

Women are much less able than previously 'disadvantaged' workers to identify with 'advantaged' workers and to follow their model in the transition to stable work. Further, the social definition of family and sex roles continues to undercut employment stability among women. And as the percentage of women in the labor force continues to increase, some employers seem more and more likely to move many jobs into the secondary market in response to the (expected) behavioral characteristics of secondary women employees. (Gordon, 1972, p. 48)

Women, like other disadvantaged workers, become aware that they have been preselected for the secondary labor market since they do not rise in a way commensurate with their education and skills or performance. They lose their motivation; the view of them as secondary becomes a self-fulfilling prophecy.

Some hold that by luring more and more women into paid work capitalism has been undermining its own interest in unpaid labor, and is whittling away at patriarchal authority as well. The argument is made that as more of the housewife's services are available commercially or are provided by the welfare state the housewife is being liberated and the power of patriarchal control undercut.

It is true that there is tension between the felt need of a man to be the support of his family and the need of the family for two salaries. There is tension between the need of employers for women's services in the home and for women doing women's jobs on the labor market. So far the high-wire balancing act is being done by women, however. Predictions about the disappearing housewife have proved false before. 'By the early 1900s,' writes Alice Kessler-Harris (1981) of the US, 'so many tasks had been removed from the home that some people feared the home itself would disintegrate' (p. 42). The point to be emphasized is that it does not really matter if women go out to work for pay, even if they work full-time year in year out, as long as the convention remains in force that women are essentially wives and mothers and that it is they who are responsible for what goes on in the family. It is this that locates them on the occupational ladder. She may be disguised as a worker but she's really a housewife: she must be, since her husband is the breadwinner. This is what Oakley (1974) calls 'the validating myth for a social order founded on the domestic oppression of women' (p. 184). In fact, as she points out, the reverse is true; *because* women take care of children men are free to involve themselves totally in their jobs.

Woman's two roles actually reinforce each other:

The woman worker is punished at home for not giving adequate nurturant service because of her workplace responsibilities; she is punished at the workplace both for being an 'unreliable' person who may be called to her home responsibilities at any time and for being a person who at most has only 'housekeeping' skills to offer at the workplace. Thus each of her activities downgrades the other and cements her position at the bottom of the status and power hierarchies of both the public and the private sphere. (Boulding, 1976, p. v)

This equilibrium of downward pressure has been maintained with extraordinary consistency, as all studies of the division of labor in the home illustrate. The very fact that the number of hours a woman spends on housework has not decreased either in the UK or the US over the past fifty years (Oakley, 1974; Strober, 1976) testifies to the fact that the 'validating myth' is constantly being infused with new power.

If less time is spent on cooking today, more is spent on shopping, home management, maintenance and child care. This is only partly due to higher standards – the explanation usually given. The content of the housewifely role is constantly changing. The role of capitalism in creating an artificial demand for products and appliances and multiplying the housewife's tasks through the creation of a consumer society mentality has often been stressed. The expenditure of UK consumers on services declined between 1954 and 1974 in spite of an increase in income; what increased was the purchase of consumer goods that replace services. Technology then imposes its own tyranny; if you have a pasta-making machine you must make your own pasta. Technology has also resulted in women taking over entirely jobs previously performed or shared by other members of the family. Urban pollution has increased demands on housecleaning; many housewives function as family chauffeurs; jobs like decorating and sewing are returning to the home because of the high cost of professional work; welfare cuts have increased family responsibility for the elderly and the chronically ill, and this responsibility almost inevitably falls on women (Bose, 1979; Arnold et al., 1981; Leira, 1983; Rothschild, 1981; J. W. Scott, 1982; Weinbaum and Bridges, 1979).

Nona Y. Glazer (n.d.) has been looking at the way

capitalism is shifting onto the housewife work that was formerly done by paid personnel and thus, as she puts it, directly appropriating women's unpaid labor. She has studied this particularly in the way retail buying is being transformed into a self-help experience in the US. Instead of the convenience of phoning in her order, dropping off a shopping list, sending one of the children, or having a sales clerk explain the merchandise, the shopper in the ubiquitous self-service market or department store must do advance consumer research to inform herself of the use, qualities and relative advantages of hundreds of competing products. She must locate the goods herself, determine the price, study the fine print, and in the case of food must unload it at the check-out counter and often load it on the other side. She must transport it by car, often long distances, and unload it and store it at the other end. A new inconvenience to the consumer is the introduction of price scanners at check-out counters and the accompanying elimination of price tags on individual items in many US supermarkets. Time gained at the cashier's desk is lost as the shopper has to search the shelves for price markers.

Moreover, as the consumer has taken over from the trained male clerk, whose job had some prestige and could earn him commissions, the latter has been replaced by low-paid, untrained, frequently part-time female cashiers (an example of how jobs are restructured for women and downgraded into the 'secondary' labor market).

Heidi Hartmann (1981a) has summarized recent time-use studies made in the US and finds neither a decrease in time spent on housework nor a more equal division of tasks in the family. She concludes that wives do an average of 70 per cent of work in the home, husbands 15 per cent, and children the rest. All research points in the same direction. The wife is largely responsible for child care; the husband's contribution remains about the same whatever the family size, and does not increase very much if his wife takes a job outside the home. A woman who does not work for wages spends a *minimum* of forty hours a week caring for home, husband and children, thirty hours if she has a paid job. Hartmann also concludes that time spent on housework by wives and husbands does not vary very much by economic class or ethnic group.

The same pattern prevails across national boundaries. In spite of policies that encourage greater participation by men in family life in Sweden, a study made in 1976 in families where both husband and wife were gainfully employed revealed that 67 per cent of wives did all the cooking, 80 per cent did all the laundry, and 53 per cent did all the cleaning (Scott, 1982a). According to a 1983 report by the Swedish Ministry of Labor, women spend thirty-five hours weekly on housework, men between seven and eight.

The UNESCO sponsored Multinational Time-Budget Research Project carried out in 1965–6 in twelve countries (seven in Eastern Europe, three in Western, Peru and the US) found the same characteristic division of household labor in countries at varying stages of industrial development, with different socio-economic systems and different labor market participation rates for women. 'The gap between the small share men tend to take at present in household tasks and the burden women have to bear in the household is far too great and no technology is in sight which could reduce the burden on women to a substantial extent,' writes the coordinator of this study (Szalai, 1976, p. 86). Women's housework serves male relatives and male planners in *all* types of industrial society.

The economic importance of women's unpaid work in the home and their other non-market activities, and the connection between these and women's poverty, becomes dramatically clear when we look at the way they function in support of the international economic order. Women in Third World countries, as we saw in the last chapter, engage in many activities besides those routinely connected with housework and children. Rural women gather wood, carry water, garden, store crops, process food and work directly in crop production on family farms supplying the market. They work without wages and the monetary rewards go to men. Women appear on the records, if they are listed at all, as unpaid family workers. This is often true of their work in crafts and trading as well. Papanek (1977) gives the example of the carpet weavers of the Middle East, who are supported by but not paid by male relatives, who put their products on the market.

These arrangements, as Papanek points out, depend on non-economic ties and have their origins in the traditional division of roles between men and women. Such relationships based on marriage and kinship also determine women's responsibility for the care not only for children and elderly parents but for assistance to other related households. With the migration of men to cash crop plantations or to factory work in towns, women in many parts of the Third World have taken over subsistence farming. They have thus become the mainstay of the welfare system that helps make Third World wage workers such a bargain for multinationals. The rural subsistence sector not only supports the worker's children and family members too old or ill to work; it takes care of the worker himself in unemployment or ill health.

This system originated under colonialism. Barbara Stuckey and Margaret Fay (1980) describe the way land expropriation and taxes were used to create a migratory labor force for the European-owned plantations and mines. Workers received just sufficient in cash and kind to keep them while they were on the job:

> Migrant labour provides the employer with a continuous supply of labour power, without his being responsible politically or accountable financially for the long-term survival of that supply. Wage employment in mines, on plantations, and in construction and transport made no provisions for illness, injury, unemployment, families, or old age. All these 'social services' were provided by the rural subsistence economy of the African and Asian villages. . . . To a much greater extent than in the 19th and 20th centuries in Europe, the employers of wage-labourers were exempted from bearing the full costs of maintaining their labourers. (p. 22)

In the colonial period the subsistence sector still included much of the male population. Today the support it offers is increasingly the responsibility of women, especially in Africa. Boserup (1970) writes: 'This burden African women take on in the manless villages is their contribution to Africa's export production. Only in a quite superficial sense can it be said that this effort is based solely on male labor' (p. 79).

A new phase of migration has begun in the past two decades, caused by the expanding acreage of highly mechanized giant farms with reduced needs for labor, and by the inability of small farmers to compete with richer local farmers who have access to technology, high-grade seeds and credits. The result has been the concentration of migrant populations in the cities and towns of the Third World. The sprawling slums around Mexico City, Buenos Aires, Sao Paulo, Rio de Janeiro, Cairo, Calcutta, Bombay – cities approaching the 10 million mark or well past it – are only the most sensational symptom of this development.

Urban growth is outstripping the possibilities for urban employment. Third World unemployment and underemployment have been put as high as 50 per cent (Sivard, 1982). Reliable figures are hard to come by because in some cases national statistics include as employed people who have worked a few days only during the year.

Opportunities for jobs in what is called the 'formal sector' are concentrated in export production for Western European, North American and Japanese firms hiring primarily male workers. Chances for women in this sector are few. Yet more and more single women and, in Latin America and Asia particularly, whole families, are moving permanently to these centers because the means of rural subsistence is rapidly shrinking.

This 'surplus population' survives primarily by supplying cheap goods and services to those who have jobs with foreign firms or with local enterprises acting as subcontractors. Because they cannot get work elsewhere, women constitute a disproportionate share of workers in the informal sectors. Since they are largely illiterate and unskilled they make up the lowest strata among these already disadvantaged. Women are usually excluded from the more profitable informal sector enterprises in which men engage: licensed selling and cottage industries requiring skills and tools. Unmarried women are most frequently employed as domestic servants. Prostitution is one of the few alternatives.

Housewives may provide domestic services for others, but this is frequently done free as family help or mutual aid. Otherwise women are largely limited to home production, often unlicensed vending, and house-to-house selling. Some engage in crafts, but they are handicapped by lack of entre- preneurial skills and credit (Arizpe, 1977; Jelin, 1977; Jules- Rosette, 1982; Little, 1976; Tinker, 1976; Youssef, 1976).

Ela Bhatt, who organized the Self-Employed Women's Association in Ahmedabad, India, reports that women are a majority of the informal sector that accounts for 45 per cent of that city's workforce. According to a survey of the associ- ation's members, 97 per cent live in slums, 93 per cent are illiterate, 91 per cent are married, and 70 per cent take their children to work with them. Some find occasional employ- ment as manual workers – head loaders or cart pullers. Another group works at home, making incense or cigarettes, or producing cheap garments or quilts on rented sewing machines using waste cloth from the textile mills. A third category comprises vendors of fruit, vegetables and eggs. No labor laws apply to these women, and they are at the mercy of money lenders to keep their enterprises going (Kneerim and Shur, n.d.).

By subsisting on the margin of life themselves, workers in the informal sector sell their goods and services at prices which make it possible for those currently employed in the formal sector to exist on their earnings. They are, in the argument of Stuckey and Fay (1980), the modern version of the rural subsistence sector:

> The past, necessary reliance of Third World wage-earners on their family members working in the traditional rural subsistence sector, without whose labour the low-paid wage-worker could not have survived, is being re-established inside the cities. What is called the growth of the informal sector is in fact the movement – the relocation, the migration – of the rural subsistence sector into the towns. . . . (p. 38)

Women's unpaid labor in the home and out of it, besides being advantageous to men as individuals, directly and in- directly supplies services and products that no economy is

prepared to pay for. We have seen how unpaid work perpetuates the possibility of using women as a cheap paid
workforce in labor-intensive occupations where it is particularly desirable to keep labor costs down, and how women fit
into an indigenous 'welfare system' which helps to maintain
low wages throughout the economy in less developed countries. To break out of this bind women need the power to
influence policy. If they are not destined by biology to spend
their lives in a state of dependence on men, by what sudden or
gradual process have they been excluded from resources and
decision making – those ingredients essential for climbing
out of poverty?

Chapter 5

WAS IT ALWAYS THAT WAY?

How did women come to be excluded from economic opportunity and from the corridors of power? There are at least two ways of looking at women's history. One could be called the 'steady march of progress' approach. The other maps a zigzag path, full of contradictions, often appearing to turn back on itself.

The view of history as progressing from lower to higher and from worse to better is the one we are used to. The idea of progress seems irresistible to us; to doubt its inevitability is vaguely blasphemous. According to this optimistic graph, progress is equated with the development of democratic institutions expressing the fundamental equality of all humankind and with the conquest of nature by science and technology. Western woman, in the model popularized by influential social scientists, has made unprecedented strides in recent decades thanks to modernization, urbanization and technology. From being man's chattel she has (almost) become man's equal under the law. She has acquired the right to education and to political participation; and the mechanization of housework, coupled with a more democratic view of woman's potential, is at last making it possible for her to leave the seclusion of the home and to take part in economic life and public activity.

Representative of this school of thought is the respected anthropologist Raphael Patai (1967). Introducing a collection of essays written mostly by women, called *Women in the Modern World*, he wonders, in a preface bursting with goodwill toward the female sex, how it is that while man has advanced in every other field he neglected for so long to do anything about women: 'The status of women in Europe and

America as recently as the nineteenth century differed only in insignificant detail from that of Near Eastern women of four or five thousand years earlier' (p. 3). Now, however, women's liberation has arrived, thanks to Western values, 'before which all countries of the world must eventually give way. . . . All these changes, whether in technology, industrialization, urbanization, labor relations, political organization, or social structure, bring with them concomitant changes in the position of women' (p. 16). This, in Patai's view, is the only way out for all the women of the world:

> Every step women take in the direction of equal rights and other improvements in their position, must inevitably lead them away from the traditional culture of their society and toward a Westernized or partly Westernized cultural configuration. In this sense, all women who fight for emancipation fight for modernism and Westernism.' (p. 17)

From this perspective, woman has no history. She has simply stepped from thousands of years of darkness into the light. Thanks to Western values men have finally decided to extend a helping hand to women.

A second view, now gaining recognition, sees the history of women as being as thickly layered and richly patterned as that of men. While recorded history does not reveal any periods or societies in which women have held more power than men, women's status has varied widely from age to age, from country to country, from class to class, and defies efforts to reduce it to a formula (Bridenthal and Koonz, 1977; Carroll, 1976). It is impossible to square the vast compendium of women's activities from Neolithic times to the present assembled by Elise Boulding (1976), with its frieze of women toolmakers and builders, innkeepers, shopkeepers, hairdressers, queens, priestesses, judges, administrators, warriors, church officials, scholars and traders, or Sheila Rowbotham's revolutionaries and reformers (1972, 1973), with a static view of women passively confined to the house for four or five millenia.

One thing this history confirms is that modernization and technology do not treat women and men the same way. We have already looked at some of the evidence for this.

Historians who focus on women's activities, moreover, point to a discontinuity between women's legislative gains and their economic and political power. While it is true that many legal limitations on women have been removed or mitigated in recent decades, this should be cause for embarrassment rather than jubilation, since most of the changes in civil law have secured for women 'benefits' that men have taken for granted for decades if not for centuries. The fact that Italian wives can now take a paid job without their husband's permission, that a British married woman may choose her domicile, a French woman may open a bank account even if her husband says no, a German wife has a voice in the education of her children – these changes are recognition that the previous state of affairs long ago lost its real importance for anyone.

Besides, not all these legal improvements represent a break with the Dark Ages or with 4000-year-old tribal custom, but are reversals of some of the more modern stringent limitations set by English Common Law or, on the European continent, in conformity with the Napoleonic Code of 1804. Of the former, E. S. Turner (1966) writes:

> The Common Law of England, in the early part of the nineteenth century, granted a wife fewer rights than had been accorded her under later Roman law, and hardly more than had been conceded to an African slave before emancipation. . . . [Her husband] owned her body, her property, her savings, her personal jewels and her income, whether they lived together or separately. He could deprive her of her assets entirely as he thought fit, and he could do this whether he were alive or dead. . . . Under the old English law there could be no doubt that a woman succeeded on equal terms, with women of other nations, to the property of her husband. . . . The decrees of legal tribunals, however, had abrogated this old law and by imperceptible degrees had deprived married women of their rights, while allowing husbands to deal with the property of their wives as they saw fit.' (pp. 135, 137)

During the 1970s more than twenty-five countries gave women greater equality in the family, true, 'but progress slows to a snail's pace when money and power are at stake, as they are in the labor market and the political arena' (Newland, 1979, p. 18).

One solid victory that women would appear to have won is the right to vote and to stand for office. Worldwide, 99.5 per cent of women can now participate in the political process; seventy-four countries have granted female suffrage since 1945. Yet this has hardly enhanced their political influence. In the political arena figures like Mrs Gandhi and Mrs Thatcher appear more like aberrations than trends. With few exceptions women make up less than 10 per cent of national legislative bodies (less than 5 per cent in the UK and the US). The exceptions include socialist countries, where real power resides not in parliament or local administrative bodies, but in the highest echelons of the Communist Party.

Fluctuations render small gains meaningless. West Germany had 10 per cent female members in the Bundestag in 1950, only 6.8 per cent in 1975. In Sweden, which tops the list of countries with 25 per cent female parliamentary membership, Birgitta Wistrand, a leading feminist, says: 'Now that women are in politics the power has moved to the trade unions where there are few women and to the employers where there are no women' (H. Scott, 1982a, p. 161). Lenelotte von Bothmer (1978), a long-time member of the West German parliament, describes the powerlessness of women who do make it to the legislative halls: lacking an old-girl network and the backing of powerful interests they are 'in large measure without political influence. The internal decision-making process takes place without them. Their advice and opinions are worth nothing' (p. 105).

As far as economic power is concerned, historians who have examined women's position over the centuries trace an actual decline in status during the 250 years from the middle of the seventeenth century to 1900, encompassing the rise of capitalism and the Industrial Revolution. The invention of the steam engine accelerated a process that makes it possible to fly to the moon. The same process separated the domains of men and women into 'public' and 'private' and created the conditions for the full-time housewife. Capitalism did not invent patriarchy, the nuclear family, or the institutionalized personal domination of women by men, nor is it responsible for the idea of 'men's work' and 'women's work.' It made good use of what it found, however, and one of industrialization's products is the stay-at-home wife who, alone in a money economy, performs without pay production tasks that cannot be profitably taken over by the market. By this 'modernization' process women were separated for the first time in history from the production of material wealth.

Most of what we know about women in the 'Dark Ages' comes from ancient legal documents and thus tells us about the lives of high-born women primarily. Far from being passive or invisible, these women were highly visible and frequently played an important economic role. Roman law and Christianity, both of which held women to be naturally inferior, were imported into tribal northern Europe by the Roman armies, but their influence was felt slowly and unevenly in the sparsely populated kingdoms that emerged after the defeat of the West Roman Empire in A.D. 476. To the barbarian peoples law was custom, and custom was locally interpreted. The historian David Herlihy (1971) notes that 'medieval religion, law and science left the position of women quite loosely, even ambiguously defined' (p. 4).

Women played an 'extraordinary' role in the management of family property – the main source of wealth – in the Middle Ages, and it is clear that in many cases they not only managed it but had the right to dispose of it. Thousands of charters recording dealings in land – sales, leases, gifts – survive for the period 700–1200 in Europe, and according to those examined by Herlihy in one out of ten cases the land was transferred by a woman in her own right and name.

When the Crusades emptied Europe of warrior knights in the twelfth century, wives managed, bought, sold, collected rents and became powers in territories and kingdoms. The deaths of many of these fighting men contributed to the accumulation of land in the hands of women. Herlihy (1976) puts the proportion of land held by women in the twelfth century as high as 18 per cent in Spain, and 12 per cent in Germany. In some cases noble ladies had great power, including the right to mint money, appoint church officials and raise armies. They even led their troops in person, wearing armor, and in France particularly a strong tradition of female military leaders developed (Casey, 1976). Thus Joan of Arc, when she appeared in the fourteenth century, was not the anomaly she seems to us.

Education was for the few in the Middle Ages, but there is no doubt that among those who benefited were aristocratic women. Some of these were celebrated by the fourteenth-century Italian poet Christine de Pisan, who was herself educated in France. Outraged by the ignorance and prejudice of men as far as women were concerned, she wrote an allegory entitled *City of Ladies*, depicting a city built by women for all the famous women of legend and history. From her as well as from other sources we know that 'ladies and baronesses who lived on their lands' had to be able to read and calculate in order to administer their own and their husband's estates (Herlihy, 1971, p. 8).

Many women who did not marry shared in both power and knowledge in the early Middle Ages by joining one of the religious orders that prospered with the spread of Christianity, as wealthy barons concerned about the future of their souls made gifts to the church. These religious institutions, because of their positions, wielded great secular influence as well as being the sole repositories of literature and learning. Women played the leading role in the double monasteries, religious communities of both men and women. St Hilda, for example, established the double monastery at Whitby in the seventh century, the first abbess to preside over such an institution in England, and 'the most learned female before the Conquest' (Leibell, 1971). The Benedictine Abbey of Fontevrault in France was ruled for 600 years by a succession of abbesses who controlled its enormous wealth and were directly answerable to the pope (Gage, 1972).

Female orders, too, exercised economic power. Consider the Chatteris nunnery in south-east England, founded in 970, which survived until the dissolution of the monasteries in England by Henry VIII in 1538. The Chatteris manor must have been typical of hundreds of the more modest religious institutions. By 1200 the abbess presided over 1500 acres, comprising five villages where her word was law 'for almost everything short of murder and treason' (Parker, 1975, p. 59).

Women were involved to a remarkable degree in the only outlet for opposition to the medieval Establishment – the heretical sects that appeared in the twelfth century. The church reforms of the eleventh century, which insisted on the celibacy of the clergy and abolished the double monasteries, deprived women of influence. At the same time the center of learning moved from the monasteries to the cathedral schools and universities which excluded women. In contrast, the heretical sects appealed to women. Chief among these was the Beguines, a religious community of women which had no formal rules and exacted no vows. They drew large numbers of women who were doomed to remain single for lack of a dowry, fed them, taught them to read the Gospel, and permitted them to perform religious offices. In Cologne alone, according to Herlihy (1971), some 100 houses accommodating a total of 1000 women were formed in the 100 years between 1250 and 1350.

The consolidation of the church's power and the centralization of state authority in the hands of royal houses created a hierarchical order beginning in the twelfth century that eventually deprived noble women of most of their power. Women might be involved in the management of estates, but great families restricted women's rights to inherit property in order to prevent the division of land and its transfer to other dynasties (Casey, 1976; McNamara and Wemple, 1977). 'In general most upper class women were almost entirely without political or juridical rights,' writes Catherine Hall (1980, p. 51) of fourteenth-century England. An aristocratic woman's chief function was to transmit property through marriage and to produce male heirs.

While English Common Law now applied to the nobility, farmers and artisans were still governed by custom regulated by public opinion. The expansion of trade in the thirteenth century stimulated the growth of towns and created a growing market for goods produced in family workshops. The wives of master craftsmen assisted them and took over their work when they died. According to Hall (1980), women figure in fourteenth-century English records as barbers, furriers, carpenters, saddlers, joiners and in many other trades.

Rules concerning women's membership in guilds varied and it was exceptional in mixed guilds for women to be trained as apprentices, but many learned the trade informally in their families. In Frankfurt between 1320 and 1500 there were 200 occupations in which women were engaged. Guilds also existed to protect women from male competition. All-women guilds in France in the seventeenth century included seamstresses, dressmakers, combers of hemp and flax, embroiderers, hosiers, fan and wig makers, milliners and cloak makers. Similar women's guilds existed in England (Tilly and Scott, 1978).

Peasant women in feudal Europe worked on manorial estates under the same conditions as men. They labored in the fields and mines, worked as dairymaids or domestic servants. They were bound to their husbands under the authority of the lord of the manor. Yet it appears that there was less difference between men's and women's wages in agriculture in the Middle Ages than there was in later centuries:

> The traditional work of women did not at any time before the 17th century have anything like the economically marginal character it has since acquired. . . . Most women were rural cultivators who shared almost all seasonal work with men. Only toward the end of the Middle Ages did wage differentials become pronounced, reserving to men the areas of greatest gain, such as the harvesting of wheat. This took place as wool, cereals, and wine became cash products, responsive to a rising market. In the 13th century there seems to have been little material difference between the day rates for a planter of beans, a woodcutter, or a reaper, despite the traditional segregation of some of these jobs according to sex. (Casey, 1976, p. 228)

The French sociologist Evelyn Sullerot (1976) adds:

> In the twelfth century, the female wage was approximately eighty per cent of male remuneration, by the end of the fourteenth century, it had shrunk to seventy-five percent,

and in the fifteenth century it was no more than half. In the sixteenth century, despite the growth of humanism, the increased affluence, the faster circulation of gold and the fact that work was considered valuable in itself rather than a necessary evil, women who did the same job as men received only forty per cent of their wages. (p. 35)

The scope of women's work began to narrow markedly in the seventeenth century. Women's domestic work in rural England in the early part of the century, as chronicled by Alice Clark (1982) in a now-classic study first published in 1919, could still include brewing, dairy work, the care of poultry and pigs, the production of fruit and vegetables, and the spinning of flax and wool. Significantly, her responsibilities also covered doctoring and nursing. On a farm of any size she had servants to manage, took produce to market, and habitually acted for her husband in financial matters.

On smaller farms, where the husband supplemented the family income with wage work, wives were also employed outside the home in seasonal agriculture, and could be taken on for any kind of job not excluding shearing sheep or thatching roofs. Women of all classes, and children too, were heavily involved in producing yarn or thread for the growing woollen and linen industries. About one million people, the majority women and children, were employed in weaving woollen cloth, one of the chief sources of Crown revenues. At the same time men of all classes gave time to the care and education of their children.

Among the ranks of tradesmen and early mercantile capitalists were many women who engaged in business with their husbands or who themselves owned and managed businesses. If a woman were widowed she was usually appointed the executrix of her husband's estate, while 'custom universally secured to her the possession of his stock, apprentices and goodwill . . .' (p. 293).

As the century wore on and the demands of trade increased, the division of labor became more specialized, workshops grew in size and in the capital involved. The rules of work became formalized and it was less usual to involve the wives and daughters of master craftsmen. It was also harder

to combine work and housework, and to have children under-
foot. New guild organizations jealously guarded the competitive position of their members and women were crowded
out of many trades, including such a popular female occupation as brewing, by the end of the century.

At the same time as the first leisured ladies appeared –
the wives of successful capitalists and farmers who now
devoted themselves exclusively to domestic pursuits – the
law closed in on married women. 'In order to secure complete
liberty to individual men,' writes Alice Clark (1982), the new
laws 'destroyed the collective idea of the family, and deprived
married women and children of the property rights which
customs had hitherto secured to them' (p. 237).

Class differences sharpened, with particular consequences for women. The latter part of the seventeenth and
the beginning of the eighteenth centuries saw increased
concentration of property in the hands of large landowners,
more efficient farming methods requiring considerable
capital, rising prices and heavy taxes. These accompanied
the spread of enclosure acts which deprived poor farmers of
the use of common grazing lands. The consequence was the
destruction in England of small, self-sufficient freeholders
and the pauperization of a whole class of cottagers who lived
by domestic industry – women spinning, men weaving – who
grew their own food and supplemented their income with
agricultural labor. The 'free labor' for the Industrial
Revolution was created (Morton, 1957).

The position of women was particularly acute. In the best
of times the wife of a cottager could scarcely nourish her
children, while her husband was at least fed by his employer
when he worked. If he died or deserted her she was thrown on
the mercy of the parish (Clark, 1982). As the landless poor
grew, poor rates rose and wages fell. The workhouse
appeared in the eighteenth century as a way of reducing poor
relief costs and forcing the unemployed to take jobs under any
conditions. Inmates worked for their maintenance; children,
especially, were taught a trade, and such 'pauper apprentices' were later transported by the thousands to mill towns
as industrial labor, clothed, fed and housed by the mill
owners under such scandalous conditions that the first of a

series of bills limiting the use of children was passed in 1802 (Morton, 1957; Piven and Cloward, 1982).

Next to children women were the ideal textile employees because their already vulnerable economic and social position made them ready to accept almost any wages. Women were also found in the coal mines, in the light metal trades (cutlery, nails, needles, chains) and in the glass industry, together with many children. Women's limited alternatives were sweated labor in shirtmaking, dress-making or milliners' establishments or as domestics, while men were hired in the growing iron and steel industry, in railroads, canal and road building and other construction.

Frederick Engels (1953) complained in *The Condition of the Working Class in England* in 1845 that of 420,000 factory operatives in the British Empire in 1839 more than half were female, while less than one-quarter were adult males. In fact, women over 18 made up less than one-third of this workforce, the rest being boys and girls. Probably a small minority were married women. According to figures cited by Strachey (1930), of 125,000 workers employed in Lancashire cotton mills in 1833, 65,000 were women, of whom only 10,000 were married, although much was made by reformers, Engels in-cluded, of the threat to the home represented by the employ-ment of mothers. Similarly the highly publicized plight of women in the mines (according to the census of 1841 only 2350 women and girls were working underground) disguised, whether intentionally or otherwise, the much more wide-spread negative impact of industrialization on women. Strachey (1930) summarizes the fall in women's status:

> The Industrial Revolution began long before the nineteenth century; and all through its course it was accompanied by a decline in the economic importance of women. Their change from partners to parasites was an exceedingly far-reaching social phenomenon, and their collapse from skilled workers to cheap labourers added greatly to the confusions and disasters which accompanied industrial development. As the change proceeded it wrenched away from women great portions of their traditional work, and thus forced them either to

follow it into the labour market, or sit in idleness at home.
(p. 52)

By the later nineteenth century, in France as well as
England, the separation of home and workplace had eliminated married women, especially mothers, from most of the
more productive factory jobs available to women, and single
women and children largely replaced them as supplementary
family wage earners. In England in 1911 less than 10 per cent
of married women were gainfully employed compared to 68
per cent of single women (Tilly and Scott, 1978).

In colonial America survival depended as much on women's
labor as on men's. Food, clothing, furniture, soap, candles,
linen cloth, medicine – almost everything was made at home.
Families bartered their services and their surpluses. Women
took part in pitching hay and ploughing, men helped their
wives at the loom. British laws prohibiting the colonies from
trading with each other, the inability to pay for imported
British goods, and finally the boycott of British products
perpetuated home manufacture. In the towns, although
excluded from guilds, women engaged in crafts with their
fathers or husbands, ran shops and inns, brewed beer. Slave
women worked at heavy labor as a matter of course.

Yet under eighteenth-century Anglo-American law,
while a spinster, or *femme seule*, had the same rights as a
man except for the vote, a married woman, a *femme couverte*,
merged her identity with her husband's; they were one, and
he was that one. The wife's property and earnings belonged to
him; she could not make a will or bring a lawsuit without
him; in case of legal separation she lost her right to her
children. As in Britain, it was not until the end of the nineteenth century that married women in most of the original
thirteen states had a right to their own property and earnings
(Cott, 1978; Flexner, 1979; Kessler-Harris, 1981).

Children aged 9 and 10 were also the first workers in
American textile plants. Unlike England, the US did not
have a pool of 'free labor.' Farming was the major occupation,
and it was hard to get either men or married women off the
farm. The first New England factories appealed to farm

families to send their unmarried daughters to the mills to learn hard work and discipline and put something aside for the future, but this marriage of profits and morality was short-lived. In the textile mills of Lowell, Massachusetts, women's top weekly wage was $4 compared to $12 for men. Conditions in the boarding houses where the young women were required to live were strict and miserable. Within a few years mill girls were striking against long hours and low wages in many northern cities.

By 1840 more than half of factory operatives were women (although only 10 per cent of adult women were actually employed in the paid labor force). Yet in spite of the fact that women were available and were eminently attractive to employers as cheap labor, eventually penetrating the shoe, tobacco, printing and other male trades, they had a limited future in industry. A decade later American-born women had been replaced by immigrant women; even less demanding, they could be exploited with impunity as they had little standing in the community. The chief occupations left for a 'respectable lady' were teaching and dressmaking.

In 1900 only 17 per cent of women worked for wages outside agriculture, and of these 40 per cent were servants or service workers, and only about one-quarter were in factories – the vast majority in clothing and textiles. In 1920 the female participation rate was 20 per cent due to the expansion of clerical work, but two-thirds of gainfully employed women were poor blacks or immigrants (Flexner, 1979; Kessler-Harris, 1981). According to Brownlee (1979), only slightly more than 6 per cent of American-born white married women were in the labor force compared to 7 per cent of foreign-born and 32 per cent of black wives.

Events had paralleled those in England and northern Europe. With increased productivity and the rise of an urban middle class came the new individualism and the success ethic. The ideal bride brought her husband a substantial dowry to which she lost all rights on her wedding day. His role was to succeed in business, hers to be a submissive helpmeet. Isolated from the temptations of the evil world she, like her predecessor, the aristocratic landowner's lady, produced legitimate heirs for new family dynasties built on commercial and banking fortunes rather than on wealth in land.

The 'leisured' wife was a badge of achievement, the ornament to hard work and virtue for families on the way up. While not everyone could hope to amass a fortune, everyone could aspire to a lifestyle built on the cult of motherhood and of the helpless woman incapable of managing her own affairs, destined by God to serve her husband and to 'raise children in ways that were consistent with godly values and yet not inconsistent with the need to earn a living in a godless and competitive world' (Kessler-Harris, 1981, p. 38). Although the majority of Americans still lived on farms in 1900 and the new pattern could be adopted by a relatively small class, the glorified homemaker became the public ideal.

Poor women, married and single, had these middle-class aspirations pressed on them, and in accepting them lost sight of their own best interests. Because of the increased productivity made possible by machinery, production no longer needed to involve the majority of women as full-time year-round workers. Employers saw the advantage of using women as casual labor, to undercut men, to act as strikebreakers. Kessler-Harris (1981) writes:

> The belief that women belonged at home permitted employers to exploit working women by treating them as though their earnings were merely supplemental. Until the end of the nineteenth century, women customarily received about one third to one half of the prevailing male wage, a sum seldom sufficient even for a single woman to support herself. . . . Department store managers refused to engage salesclerks who did not live in families, for fear that financial need would drive them to prostitution. Employers who were convinced that women belonged at home refused to train them to perform skilled jobs, exacerbating their poverty. . . . (pp. 63–4)

A major share of the responsibility for the marginalization of women and the establishment of occupational segregation under industrial capitalism rests with the trade unions. This was true in Britain, in the US, and in the European unions, not excluding those affiliated to the international socialist labor movement (Foner, 1947; Hartmann, 1981b; Kessler-Harris, 1981; Rowbotham, 1972; Strachey, 1930; Thönnessen, 1973).

With some honorable exceptions, they reacted to the ominous threat of cheap labor that undercut their own wages not by organizing women but by striking to prevent their hiring. They wrote provisions into their constitutions preventing women from joining. They refused training to women, threatening expulsion to any member who instructed women in the trade. When women organized themselves, national unions refused to admit them. The protective legislation for which they pressed effectively excluded women from many male occupations. Men preferred to fight for a 'family wage' rather than extend their class solidarity to women who needed jobs. 'We cannot drive the females out of the trade,' said Adolph Strasser, President of the Cigar Makers International, 'but we can restrict their daily quota of labor through factory laws' (Hartmann, 1981b, p. 162).

Over time men everywhere succeeded in reserving for themselves the jobs that were made more productive by machinery, therefore better paying. They left to women those where technology fragmented the process and allowed the use of home workers and unskilled operators. The present division of the labor force is so strikingly similar throughout the industrialized world that one feels justified in assuming that it is equally satisfactory to unions and employers.

Women have always worked, history tells us, and they have worked at all kinds of jobs. But they have rarely had enough control over the product of that work to change their own position in a decisive way. Western modernization – the proliferation of technology, and the substitution of wealth acquired by trade and manufacture for aristocratic wealth based on land inheritance – opened up undreamed-of possibilities for material comfort for everyone, yet created poverty in the midst of plenty. It ushered in a new concept of human rights, yet restricted woman's autonomy and increased their economic dependence. At the same time it conferred power of

incalculable dimensions on men – and on some men in particular – thereby vastly enlarging rather than narrowing the
gap between the sexes.

Chapter 6
WHY MEN RUN THE MACHINES

Men's control over tools, over technology, appears to have put in his hands the power to say how society should be ordered. Women today leave the home economically naked: they not only do not own the tools, but they do not know how to operate them, do not understand their operation, and certainly have virtually no control over how they are used. Why was it women who were crowded out?

Conventional wisdom long had it that there was something about male biology that programmed the emergence of Man-the-Tool-Maker-and-User in prehistory. On closer examination it has turned out that this assumption is another strongly rooted but relatively recent part of our cultural heritage. The typical Victorian-style prehistoric family in which the male went forth to hunt while his woman and her young huddled in a cave was very much the product of the nineteenth-century origins of anthropology.

It was simply taken for granted that the division of labor in the Stone Age was just like our own. Even Frederick Engels (1972), in his attempt to counter the prevailing nineteenth-century belief in a universal, eternal and natural male domination with his own reconstruction of a prehistoric egalitarian society, assumed in *The Origin of the Family, Private Property and the State* (first published in 1884) that, 'They are each master in their own sphere, the man in the forest, the woman in the house' (p. 218). What made him think so?

A contemporary account of the evolution of human society, *The Ascent of Man* by Jacob Bronowski (1973), 'a spectacular bestseller,' based on an equally popular TV series, tells us that the first tool, a chipped stone, was a meat-eater's tool, the forerunner of the hunting weapon; that for at least a million years 'man' lived as a forager and hunter, and that this continued up to 10,000 years ago when 'he' began to domesticate animals and cultivate some plants. Woman is mentioned for the first time (and almost the last time) in his book at year 10,000 B.C. as the mother of male nomads and warriors. How did 'he' manage it all? What were the women doing for more than a million years?

Primatology, right down to the present time, has interpreted human society as the evolutionary consequence of the hunting nature and natural competence of our male ancestors (Haraway, 1978). Recently, however, this 'bias in both the collecting and analysis of data' has begun to be recognized even by anthropologists who were responsible for it. Evidence very similar to that used to stress the masculine origins of civilization has been adduced to produce a different reconstruction of the way human society evolved, stressing female foraging activities and women's share in the development and use of tools (Tanner and Zihlman, 1976; Zihlman, 1978).

Studies of primates provide reasons to believe in a very early division of activities between the sexes and the prevalence of sharing. Co-reviewing a recent collection of articles on these themes, *Woman the Gatherer* (Dahlberg, 1981), Prof. Sherwood Washburn, the primatologist 'most immediately associated with the man-the-hunter hypothesis' (Haraway, 1978, p. 41) acknowledges:

> The basic problem with the traditional view of man the hunter was that it hardly took account of the social system in which early human beings lived. But we have since come to see that the central problem in tracing evolution is understanding how human beings adapt through their organizations and customs. . . . It should by now be clear that women have always been important in all social systems – and perhaps especially so in foraging societies. (Washburn and Ranieri, 1981, pp. 59, 61).

Certainly the importance of 'organization and customs' for the division of labor in modern 'simple' societies living by hunting and foraging or by horticulture (pre-plough agriculture) has been thrown into relief by the immense diversity of the findings brought to light in the past ten or fifteen years by anthropologists seeking to discover how male dominance arises.

The experience of these societies is relevant not because it can tell us how people lived and thought 50,000 years ago; it can't. These are contemporary societies and not cultural fossils. All have been influenced in some way by contact with industrialized society. What they can tell is how tasks are distributed in communities that do not share our technologies, ideas of religion, government, property, justice, do not read our books and newspapers, do not watch our TV or go to our psychiatrists. If anthropologists could agree on how to interpret the evidence – or indeed on what the evidence is – we might yet learn how power and prestige come to be divided between men and women. We are still in the stage of many hypotheses, however (Rapp, 1979; Strathern, 1981).

There appears to be general agreement in one area: we cannot deduce from these societies that control of technology is inevitably male. The division of tasks by sex appears to be a universal organizing principle, but from the extraordinary variety in the way the work is allotted it is clear that the meaning of 'maleness' and 'femaleness' is not read out from the biological differences but is given by society itself.

'Mother' does not have the same content for all hunters and gatherers. 'Even the process of reproduction is subject to social construction,' writes La Fontaine (1981). 'In many societies it is men not women who are credited with reproductive powers ... the significant psychological event is ejaculation' (p. 336). By the same token, man's 'physical strength relative to women may be culturally constructed into "natural" aggressiveness as a hunter or killer' (p. 342). Among the Hadza of Tanzania, for instance, boys and old men use small bows for hunting which women could also easily employ but never do because women's work is defined as food gathering. Women may kill small game with their digging sticks but this is not considered 'hunting.'

Women in 'simple' societies contribute the bulk of the diet, either as gatherers or as horticulturists, besides bringing home small game. They are by no means the 'weaker sex.'

Much of the heavy work falls to them. They often build the shelters; usually they are the water carriers and the burden bearers. The tasks of food processing and preparation are also theirs.

In some societies the division of labor is extreme, in others men's and women's occupations overlap. While it is true that long-distance hunting and metal working (weapon making) are almost always the responsibility of men, while infant care, cooking and vegetable gathering are the province of women, women in some societies hunt and fight with the same success as men. The Agta women of the Philippines are 'superb hunters,' exchanging some of the deer, pig and monkey that they bring down for corn and rice (Estioko-Griffin and Griffin, 1981). And the records show that in the West African kingdom of Dahomey in 1845 (before French colonization) women made up 5000 of the army's 12,000 warriors (Oakley, 1974).

In order to agree on who wields the power in these societies we would first have to be sure what their concept of power is. What do we mean when we talk about male dominance? As Rayna Rapp Reiter (1975) writes:

> If we only have a vague idea of what constitutes dominance, we cannot know if it reflects the experience of both men and women, or if it is instead something the men assert and the women deny. . . . In such a case, is dominance a male fantasy? An anthropological fantasy? Or an expression of the internal workings and contradictions of a system for which we only have half the pieces? It is not clear that primitive peoples dichotomize their world into power domains. Coming from an extremely hierarchical cultural milieu, we tend to construct categories to contain social differences, and then rank them in terms of power. We build master-theories out of such notions of differences, but we do not know if the oppositions and hierarchies we construct are universal or simply reflect our own experience in a class-stratified society. (p. 15)

Many anthropologists have assumed a universal separation between 'private' and 'public' domains such as is often employed to describe our Western societies (Rosaldo and Lamphere, 1974). When women's activities concerned with procreation and food are viewed as 'private' and men's activities involving rituals and hunting as 'public,' and therefore more important, the investigator almost invariably comes up with a picture of male dominance. Recent critics of this approach have pointed out that it obscures the interdependence of women's and men's activities in such societies, where there is no sharp public-private distinction in our sense. By creating a false hierarchy of functions it hides the real meaning of what people do (Rapp, 1979; Rosaldo, 1980; Nash, 1978; Stoler, 1977; Leacock, 1981a; Skar, 1979).

An alternative approach is to try to read the symbolism of people's behavior, a difficult task since apparently similar societies do not attach the same symbolic meaning to similar acts (Strathern, 1981). Using the techniques of symbolic anthropology to discover clues to how preindustrial societies create their particular 'sex-role plans,' Peggy Sanday (1981) finds that male dominance and female power vary with historical experience and natural environment. From her analysis of ethnological descriptions of 156 tribal societies, Sanday concludes that 'each culture can be shown to have different ideas about what it means to be male, what it means to be female, and how the two sexes should interact' (p. 16).

She distinguishes three broad categories. In the first, egalitarian type of society where the environment is seen as a friendly partner, women and men cooperate in many activities and women's power is stressed. An example is the Balinese, for whom the distinction between the sexes seems unimportant for daily life and men and women may act interchangeably. Their clothing is almost identical, inheritance is through both men and women, women and men function as priests. Another example is the Lepcha, an agricultural people in the Himalayas, where customs regarding the division of labor are not enforced and fathers are actively engaged in child care.

These are not unique examples. Sarah Lund Skar (1979), for example, has described a Quechua Indian village in Peru where work is totally shared, both sexes own land and animals, and both participate in decision making. Colin

Turnbull (1981) concludes from long acquaintance with the Mbuti pygmies in Zaire that theirs is an egalitarian society. Women hunt, gather, take part in rituals. The emphasis is on interdependence.

The second category describd by Sanday is a 'dual-sex configuration,' also found in predominantly plant societies. Men and women have distinctly separate but complementary domains. In one such, the Iroquois Indian tribes, women's fertility and the bounty of nature were revered and cere-monies stressed woman's food production. Women were dominant in the symbolic, economic and family spheres, men in hunting and intertribal affairs. Similarly, among the Ashanti of West Africa before British colonization male chiefs were assisted by 'queen mothers' with great powers. The Ashanti stress the vital importance of both male and female activities to survival. Sanday writes:

> When the female creative principle dominates or works in conjunction with the male principle, the sexes are either integrated and equal in everyday life or separate and equal. . . . In no sense are women portrayed as responsible for sin and the fall of man, nor are they relegated only to conception and obedience in everyday life. (p. 33)

Societies characterized by male dominance are usually those that depend primarily on animals for survival and where the environment is viewed as hostile. In these societies, says Sanday, men believe that danger is ready to strike at any time. Its source is not clear, but often it is associated with female sexuality and the power of repro-ductive functions. Men must seize their share of power lest they remain impotent before threatening chaos.

Among people in this category are the Yanomamo Indians of Venezuela and northern Brazil, 'one of the most warlike and male-oriented societies in the world' (p. 49). Female infanticide, practised to restore the balance between population and failing protein resources, results in a short-age of women and sexual jealousy. 'Cannibalism, rape and murderous revenge are responses to the tensions created by precarious existence and by the perception that the universe contains uncontrollable destructive forces' (p. 49).

Karla Poewe (1980), an anthropologist who uses a Marxist approach, also stresses the need to study the way men and women see themselves and each other, and the way these 'ideologies' interact with the society's political economy. She arrives at a range of variations very close to Sanday's. In both these models male dominance is much less common than is usually believed.

In Sanday's analysis, men are associated with big game hunting and danger, and thus with warfare, because this is consistent with the distinction people make between life giving and life taking. Men become expendable because they do not give birth; this is the cultural interpretation of the basic biological facts: 'It is easy to imagine dependence on the male world evolving when expansion, immigration, or social stress puts men in the position of fighting literally or figuratively to maintain an old or to forge a new sociocultural identity' (p. 181). Male dominance is not inevitably the outcome, but arises in societies already marked by sexual segregation. 'Mythical' male dominance occurs where women have political and economic power but allow men to act as though they were the dominant sex. Where women have accepted real male dominance, Sanday believes, it has been for the sake of social and cultural survival.

In today's world stress for subsistence societies is associated with contact with Western civilization. Another anthropologist, Felicia Ekejiuba (1977), writing about transitions that have taken place recently in the Third World, argues that 'structural and historical processes that erode the position of women and shift the balance in men's favor' – such as orthodox religions, colonization, capitalism, migration, industrialization, modernization, development –

transform male superiority and power from the symbolic and fragile to real domination by . . . making the know-ledge, skills, professions, and products of these processes first available to men. In consequence, men are placed in a position where they define these as scarce and prestigious commodities and discriminate legally and informally, through male-created myths of female inferiority, against women's participation in these processes. (p. 91)

Making use of these insights, we can hypothesize that at an earlier stage of human existence it was under the stress of competition for resources and of migration that the marginal or potential advantage men possessed in the shape of a monopoly on hunting and weapon making became real power through warfare, the spoils of war, and subsequent political and economic alliances.

Of course, not all early technology had to do with hunting and fighting. Women were certainly among the first inventors. Starting from the now widely acknowledged premise that gathering and processing vegetables was a predominantly female occupation, Autumn Stanley (1981) has summarized the evidence for women's contribution to food technology. During the 2 million years of human life that preceded the discovery of horticulture (intentional planting rather than simply gathering) women developed the digging stick, the carrying sling or bag, the first sickle, grindstones for grain, food storage containers, winnowing, grain roasting, and food preservation methods such as smoking and curing with honey.

Horticulture, which appeared in the Middle East at about the same time as the domestication of animals, around 10,000 B.C., was probably accidentally discovered by women gatherers. In the process of its development, according to Stanley's account, women invented the hoe, the spade and the simple plough used to scratch a furrow. They developed baskets, grain hullers and detoxification methods to remove bitterness, introduced fertilization, irrigation and the use of fire to clear the land. They practised crop rotation and understood the value of different types of soil. The eight most important cereals were domesticated in this period. The crank, which appeared on the early rotary hand grinder mills, is one of the cornerstones of mechanical technology, and was probably invented by women.

The sex of the cultivator changed as horticulture became agriculture. With the introduction of the iron plough (in Egypt as early as 3500 B.C.), and especially the animal-drawn plough, and of large-scale irrigation systems such as the canals built in Mesopotamia about 3000 B.C., men became predominant in the technological aspects of cultivation. What made agriculture attractive to men if they had previously attached prestige to hunting or herding? Why were women willing to relinquish their main economic role, one which gave them control over the distribution of food, a major source of power?

Most hypotheses point to the greater difficulty of combining ploughing with infant care and the time investment involved which men but not women could afford. Stanley emphasizes the direct impact of a population explosion on women's work. Settled agriculture, with its far greater productivity, offers richer nutrition, and earlier and more frequent pregnancies are a result. This effect has been noticed in contemporary foraging societies when they settle in villages and adopt a grain-based diet, as well as in historical studies of population trends.

Increased fertility would have restricted women's time and mobility at the same time that agriculture demanded more time, especially with larger populations to feed. As the increased rewards of planting, harvesting and the domestication of animals made hunting less necessary and less economical, men had more time to become farmers. Women still raised small animals and were responsible for food processing and cooking.

Agriculture increased herds. Grain supplies and cattle became political and economic resources that men could add to their control over metal working and warfare. This could have been the way patriarchal power together with male primacy in technology arose in the fertile lands of the Middle East, one of the sources of modern civilization. The picture is one of a gradual take-over, proceeding differently in different parts of the world.

Such a development would not of itself make men inevitably the exclusive architects of a technological society. Women are not entirely absent from the written records of early science and invention, although it requires some enterprise to discover their names. 'Maria the Jewess' was a first-century alchemist in Alexandria who invented laboratory instruments still in use today. Hypatia, who held the chair of mathematics and philosophy at the University of Alexandria in the fourth century, a pagan and advocate of Greek scientific rationalism, was murdered by the Christian monks of the Church of St Cyril (Alic, 1981). Women practised as physicians in the Arab world, particularly in Moorish Spain, where they attended the University of Cordova. Under Moorish influence women studied science at Italian universities as well. It took centuries of development of the Christian doctrine of women's moral inferiority before they were finally barred from the world of higher learning everywhere in Europe. August Bebel (1971) in his classic *Woman Under Socialism* quotes a decree of the faculty of the University of Bologna, passed as late as 1377:

> And whereas woman is the fountain of sin, the weapon of the devil, the cause of man's banishment from Paradise and the ruin of the old laws; and whereas for these reasons all intercourse with her is to be diligently avoided; therefore do we interdict and expressly forbid that any one presume to introduce in the said college any woman whatsoever, however honorable she be. (p. 205)

The deliberate, systematic exclusion of women from science and technology, and the use of science to establish the female sex as irrational and threatening yet fragile and passive, incapable of higher thought and thus a fit object for male dominance, dates from our modern era.

Science was in hibernation in Europe during the Middle Ages. Scholarship was for the few, and its aim was to reconcile the teachings of Christianity with the traditions of Greece and Egypt in mathematics, alchemy and astronomy. All nature was one, and science was a matter for philosophical speculation. Humanity was part of a Great Chain of Being, attached through the mind to God and through the body to the rest of the animal kingdom. All relationships were seen as deriving from this scheme (Hay, 1965).

The marriage of science and technology took place in the seventeenth century at the altar of the Industrial Revolution. The Scientific Revolution that took place between 1500 and 1700 represented a complete transformation in humankind's relationship to nature. The universe was no longer thought of as a living organism, a relationship among intelligences, but as a vast machine, an automaton composed of lifeless parts' (Ferkiss, 1974, p. 106).

Beginning with Galileo, through Bacon and Descartes to Newton, the conviction strengthened that everything important about nature could be expressed in impersonal mathematical relationships, and that it was possible to understand any phenomenon by reducing it to its components. Man was no longer part of nature but stood outside it, with the God-given right to exploit it for his needs, in Francis Bacon's words, the 'right to torture nature's secrets from her' (Capra, 1982, p. 56).

Bacon's expositions of his scientific method – experiment, deduction and further experiment – are redolent with violence and sexual imagery. Nature was a 'common harlot.' In his view:

> The new man of science must not think that the 'inquisition of nature is in any part interdicted or forbidden.' Nature must be 'bound into service,' and made a 'slave'. . . . 'Nature exhibits herself more clearly under the *trials* and *vexations* of art [mechanical devices] than when left to herself.' (Merchant, 1980, p. 169)

Bacon attributed humanity's loss of 'domination over creation' to the Fall, caused by a woman's temptation. Man had the obligation to win that power back, using inquisitorial methods suggested by the witch trials that were a feature of the reign of James I of England, in whose court Bacon served as attorney general. 'Bacon's work thus represents an outstanding example of the influence of patriarchal attitudes on scientific thought,' comments the physicist Fritjof Capra (1982, p. 56).

While Bacon contributed a new empirical method, emphasizing experimentation, Rene Descartes viewed nature as a perfect machine, governed by exact mathematical laws. Gone, as far as science was concerned, was the medieval concept according to which God, humanity and nature were inseparably linked. Plants and animals were likewise machines, and the functions of the human body could be reduced to mechanical operations (Capra, 1982). The great genius of the Scientific Revolution, Isaac Newton, combined the inductive experimental methods of Bacon and the deductive reasoning of Descartes to arrive at his concept of the entire universe as one huge mechanical system, composed of homogeneous, solid, indestructible particles. All physical phenomena were represented in the motion of these particles, which was caused by their mutual attraction, or the force of gravity. As Capra points out, the Newtonian concept worked with brilliant success in the eighteenth and nineteenth centuries, influencing all the other sciences and dominating popular understanding of the world.

While Newton provided the scientific laws that made industrialization possible, John Locke contributed the ideology of industrial capitalism. Influenced by Descartes and Newton, Locke believed that human society could be understood by examining its parts – the behavior of individuals. There were natural laws that existed independent of civil society and that entitled men to freedom, equality and property: natural rights, later to be described as the 'inalienable Rights' with which 'man is endowed by his Creator' in the American Declaration of Independence.

The state, according to Locke, was the instrument to which man voluntarily gave over these rights for safe keeping. It was the purpose of the state to foster the exploitation of nature and to protect property, because nature becomes valuable only through human industry, and 'He who appropriates land to himself by his labor does not lessen but increases the common stock of mankind' (Ferkiss, 1974, p. 28).

Rousseau's views on education, Voltaire's libertarian philosophy, the scientific humanism of Franklin and Jefferson and the *laissez-faire* economics of Adam Smith are all imbued with this rational and scientific faith in human reason and confidence in man's power over nature. Reason would triumph over authority, equality over privilege; happiness too could be attained on earth. It was through the study of nature as it was conducted by supremely rational men that woman came to be established 'scientifically' as a creature defined by her biology, like nature irrational, backward, the antithesis of reason, like nature destined to be ruled by man for the good of society (Jordanova, 1980).

We have already noted how with industrialization women were, by the end of the seventeenth century, excluded from guilds and apprenticeships, from the possibility of learning and practising trades and professions. From being butchers, bakers, candlestick makers, brewers, printers and midwives, women became spinners and housewives. That the intentional exclusion of women from general education, as it spread, and from public life was part of the new liberal political philosophy did not escape Alice Clark (1982), writing more than sixty years ago. She noted the way the new ideas had institutionalized the separation of women from men's world:

> Neither Locke, nor Hobbes, nor the obscure writers on political theory and philosophy who crowd the last half of the seventeenth century, contemplate the inclusion of women in the State of their imagination.

As the existing state still had limited functions in the seventeenth century,

> Englishmen were struggling to a realization of the other aspects of national life by means of voluntary associations for the pursuit of Science, of Trade, of Education, or other objects, and it is in these associations that the trend of their ideas is manifested, for one and all exclude women from their membership; to foster the charming dependence of women upon their husbands, all independent sources of information were, as far as possible, closed to them. (p. 303)

First among these exclusive Englishmen was, of course, Sir Isaac Newton, first among the educational institutions Cambridge University which he attended, and first among the voluntary associations was the Royal Society, which he headed from 1680 to 1704.

Clark quotes another equally prominent, eighteenth-century molder of public opinion, the poet John Milton, secretary to Oliver Cromwell:

> Milton's statement sums up very fairly the ideas of this school of thought regarding the relations that should exist between husband and wife in the general scheme of things.

They were to exist 'He for God only, she for God in him.' The
general standard of education resulting from such theories
was inevitably inferior; and the exclusion of women from
skilled industry and the professions, was equally certain to
be the consequence sooner or later, of the absence of
specialised training. (p. 304)

She might also have quoted Jean-Jacques Rousseau, the
father of modern education, who identified women as part of
nature and wanted them instructed accordingly. He wrote in
his most famous work, *Émile*:

The whole education of women ought to be relative to men.
To please them, to be useful to them, to make themselves
loved and honored by them, to educate them when young,
to care for them when grown, to counsel them, to console
them, and to make life sweet and agreeable to them – these
are the duties of women at all time. . . . (Flexner, 1979, pp.
23–4)

There were women who turned the idea of a purely masculine
scientific rationalism against its authors. Mary Wollstonecraft, a member of the community of Enlightenment
scholars, applied the mechanistic philosophy of Newton to
'prove' that when all human beings were allowed to develop
according to natural law 'female Newtons' would appear
(Magner, 1978). She was influenced by Rousseau's ideas on
how to encourage learning in children, but she remarked
acidly, 'I have probably had the opportunity of observing
more girls in their infancy than J.-J. Rousseau' (Rowbotham,
1972, p. 43); she thought that the education of women would
double the available amount of pure reason so much admired
by eighteenth-century philosophers.

She would have had to wait a century at least to test her
ideas. The nineteenth century saw the culmination of scientific justifications for keeping women in ignorance: the brain
and the womb had to compete for energy; women could not be
permitted to study, for higher education would cause the
uterus to atrophy (Ehrenreich and English, 1978).

In the US in the first half of the nineteenth century
women who wanted an education beyond the primary level

were dependent on private institutions, of which there were only a handful. Mount Holyoke College (1837) was the first to prepare young women for anything other than wifehood; Smith College, not founded until 1875, 240 years after Harvard University, was the first to insist on the same entrance requirements as those for men's institutions. Black women had to overcome a double barrier. Pioneering seminaries for young black girls were literally put to the torch, and only thirty black women had received college degrees by 1890 (Flexner, 1979; Cott, 1978).

'Higher' education in Britain for women grew out of the need to give governesses better qualifications so that poor unmarried women would be more successful in supporting themselves. Queen's College for Women and Bedford College, both founded in the 1840s, were intended to train teachers for the girls' schools that were just coming into being. Pressure on the universities to accept women began to succeed only after 1870 (Strachey, 1930). Russia followed closely upon the US in opening universities to women. On the European continent most countries began to admit them during the 1870s; only Germany waited until 1894 to award the first degree to a woman.

In spite of these obstacles, a respectable number of women actually worked in the sciences. Describing those who cautiously defied the stereotypes between 1830 and 1880 in the US, Kohlstedt (1978) names numerous pioneers who were aided by fathers or husbands, but who remained amateurs or helpmeets rather than becoming independent researchers. Others wrote textbooks, or acted as curators or librarians. 'They were encouraged to be teachers and assistants but not peers' (p. 90). An exception was Maria Mitchell, discoverer of Mitchell's comet in 1847 as a companion to her astronomer father. After being honored by the king of Denmark, she became the first woman admitted to the American Academy of Arts and Sciences, a professor at Vassar College, and a founder of the Association for the Advancement of Women.

Perhaps even more surprising are the numbers of unsung women who have made contributions in technology. Mattie Knight, for example, who patented some twenty-seven inventions in the US between 1870 and 1915 including a rotary engine, was only one of thousands of women who operated in the man's world of technology without recognition. There would be many more known women inventors were it not for the fact that they patented their processes under their husband's name because of the difficulties put in the way of a woman applying for a patent.

Today Western women theoretically have access to science and technology on the same basis as men. But aside from the various mechanisms currently employed to keep women out of male occupations that have been discussed in this book, what prevents young women from swamping the technical schools and science courses and rapidly achieving parity in participation rates? While women's education has been increasing, the gap between this education and the requirements of a highly technological society has been increasing even faster. The percentage of PhDs earned by women in all fields of science dropped between the 1920s and the mid-1960s (Fausto-Sterling, 1981). During the 1970s there were only small increases in women enrolling in mathematics and the hard sciences at the university level. In Britain few women who receive science training through secondary school or the undergraduate level survive into the upper echelons of academic science, and this is not because of the quantity or quality of their work (Martin and Irvine, 1982).

True, 'opening science to more female, minority, and handicapped students is not a major preoccupation of science educators' (Aldrich, 1978, p. 130). The problem does interest some educators, however, and women scientists in particular. Numerous studies have failed to produce real evidence of a biological distinction between the sexes that would account for difference in preference or performance (Aldrich, 1978; Fausto-Sterling, 1981; Lambert, 1978; Hubbard and Lowe, 1979; Martin and Irvine, 1982). An international comparison of results on Standard Achievement Tests in the sciences has shown that while boys do better than girls by a relatively constant margin within countries, girls in some countries do better than boys in others. Japanese girls do better than US, British, Swedish or French boys, while Hungarian girls score above Belgian boys and on a level with boys in England (Kelly and Weinreich-Haste, 1979).

The socialization of little girls in female pursuits, the association of technology with masculinity, the lack of female role models, the condescension of teachers and ridicule of male students, the prejudices of future employers – all these reasonable explanations have been given for the schools' failure to gain girls for mathematics and technical subjects. None of these seem to get at the root of the matter.

Women scientists themselves have begun to place the block at a much more fundamental level, in the conflict between the needs they believe science and technology should serve and the values that direct them today. The fact that a very limited number of women have succeeded in overcoming hurdle after hurdle simply underlines the extent to which the scientific and technological ideology that ushered in the modern era defined it as a specifically masculine endeavor.

The exclusion of the perspective of half of humanity was not a by-product but an integral part of the project. The insistence on removing women physically from the scene where science was learned, where questions were asked and hypotheses formed, where scientific ideas became technological realities and were put to particular purposes went hand in hand with the legal definition of women as nonpersons, with male control of their lives, their property and their children.

Today the hostility of the technocratic world to women is palpable. Sally Hacker (1981) spent a year investigating the ethos of engineering, which contains the smallest proportion of females of all major professions and constitutes the elite of technological society, at a prestigious US institute of technology where the interests of management and technology are intertwined. She noted that the women who had been courageous enough to enrol were not easily accepted as colleagues.

From observations and interviews she concluded that engineers are people, or become people, who find less pleasure than others in social experience and have difficulty making personal contacts. To summarize her findings:

engineers value a hierarchical organization of work, put the highest value on technological rationality and the lowest on 'womanly' qualities of intimacy and social or emotional complexity, whether in women or in men. Scatological humor and disdain are directed in lectures as well as in private conversations at women, the human body and social scientists. Scientific rationality is viewed as clean, hard, objective and capable of mathematical expression. Technical competence carries with it the right to organize and run society.

Not just the forbidding character of the education, but the aggressively competitive nature of scientific work and the elitist manner in which projects worthy of research are chosen put women at a disadvantage before they start, in the opinion of Anne Fausto-Sterling (1981). Moreover, the identification of 'objectivity' with masculinity, and the rejection of the subjective as a denial of 'reality' and at the same time typically feminine, have put women in a position where to enter the hard sciences is to deny themselves. It is not consistent with a woman's image of herself to choose science at the expense of inner experience and social relationships.

And if she does manage to be businesslike and brilliant, she still can't win. Here is how future Nobel Prizewinner James Watson (1968) describes the crystallographer Rosalind Franklin in his best-selling book *The Double Helix* — the story of the way he and Francis Crick won the race for discovery of the structure of DNA, an achievement made possible by Franklin's crucial contribution which was not acknowledged (*The New York Times*, 24 April 1983, p. 8E):

> Though her features were strong, she was not unattractive and might have been quite stunning had she taken even a mild interest in clothes. This she did not. There was never lipstick to contrast with her straight black hair, while at the age of thirty-one her dresses showed all the imagination of English blue-stocking adolescents. So it was quite easy to imagine her the product of an unsatisfied mother who unduly stressed the desirability of professional careers that could save bright girls from marriages to dull men. (p. 20)

In addition to her failure to live up to Watson's idea of

femininity, Franklin was insupportable because she persisted in acting like an independent highly qualified X-ray crystallographer, and not like somebody's assistant.

> Clearly Rosy had to go or be put in her place. The former was obviously preferable because, given her belligerent moods, it would be very difficult for Maurice [Wilkins] to maintain a dominant position that would allow him to think unhindered about DNA. . . . Unfortunately, Maurice could not see any decent way to give Rosy the boot. (pp. 20–1)

Reviewing the DNA story, Ruth Hubbard (1979), professor of biological sciences at Harvard, finds both Watson's attitude toward Franklin and the behavior of Watson and Crick in making use of Franklin's material without her knowledge to be a result, rather than a contributing cause, of the 'enormous competitiveness and secretiveness that poison the contemporary scene' of science:

> As I see it, science reached its *man*hood during the heyday of industrial capitalism when competition was hailed as the road to success in a system that was claimed to be meritocratic. Western scientists operate with the explicit assumption that competition sorts the chaff from the wheat and that genuine ability is what determines competitive success, not accidents of birth, entrepreneurial skills and/ or ruthlessness. (pp. 271–2)

One of the more important accidents of birth, of course, is the accident of being born male.

The man-the-hunter approach to toolmaking has about run its course. The premises of the Scientific and Industrial Revolutions are in crisis. The idea that there are no limits on technology, that the world can be fully understood by taking it apart and tinkering with its components, that man can stand outside nature and impose his will indefinitely has already led to depletion of non-renewable resources, extermination of other species, pollution of air and water, destruction of soil, major risks to human health and life, and finally to the possibility of total destruction. Roughly 50 billion dollars are spent annually throughout the world just on military research and development. Half of all scientists and engineers are engaged in the technology of weapon making.

At the same time the belief that women can be excluded from a direct role in the technology of the world's work has collapsed, not just because its tenets regarding women's inferiority are untrue and sex discrimination is unjust but because, as we have seen, it is economically untenable. No economy exists or can exist without woman's work, both paid work in the labor market and her ubiquitous unpaid work. Women, in turn, cannot continue to exist and support their families in the non-technological ghetto to which they have been consigned.

Chapter 7

WOMAN AS OTHER

> What particularly signalizes the situation of woman is that
> she – a free and autonomous being like all human
> creatures – nevertheless finds herself living in a world
> where men compel her to assume the status of the Other.
> (Simone de Beauvoir, 1971, p. xxix)

The hypothesis, advanced in Chapter 6, that male dominance
arose in early human societies primarily under the pressure
of hostile external circumstances has a number of advantages. It reduces the 'natural' division of labor between the
sexes (other than actual childbearing) to that necessary to
protect the lives of women-the-life-givers by assigning the
most life-endangering tasks to men. This is in turn consistent
with the fact that in modern subsistence societies studied by
anthropologists women are found in all types of work, with
the usual but not inevitable exclusion of warfare and big
game hunting, and not just those that we see as connected
with domesticity.

This scheme enables us to get along without two old
clichés: the inborn maternal instinct and innate male
aggressiveness. It permits us to recognize that men's and
women's tasks are complementary or even interchangeable
in at least some societies, instead of being arranged everywhere according to a hierarchy, with men always doing the
prestigious 'public' things and women left with the housework. This is not at all the same thing as saying that men
were naturally the ones to take up hunting because of their
superior strength, courage and brains, or that women were so
occupied with childrearing and dusting that men had to do all
the important work.

Thus this model does not make male dominance inevitable, universally prevalent since the beginning of time; it does not require us to imagine a universal defeat of women some time in prehistory. It makes the development of patriarchy, dominance and superior male prestige contingent upon a complex of concrete social conditions including historical experience, resources, environment, development, external threats – which would help to account for the variations in male/female relations in the early societies for which we have records.

Nevertheless such an explanation, even if it were more than a hypothesis, seems to tell only part of the story. The argument that men assumed the role of fighter and killer as the counterweight to women's role as lifegiver only provides a broad framework in which to look at why men have insisted on extending their authority over all spheres of life. The relentlessness with which men have urged their pre-eminence, the way every social institution has been adapted to serve that end (the state, the church, education, science), the use of physical brutality to insist on dominance in personal relationships – all this makes purely materialist advantages of female oppression seem an inadequate explanation.

What other fuel is there that propels man's drive to power over women? The non-economic or non-ideological aspects of patriarchy – those rooted in human psychology – are a relatively recent subject for study. A central place in this exploration is held by theories of sexuality and the part it plays in determining the division of labor and who exercises power.

The issue of sexuality as a source of civil power and a means of economic aggrandisement was, of course, raised by both socialists and first-wave femininists. Marx and Engels drew a connection between the unpaid prostitution of wives in bourgeois marriages contracted to protect property and the exploitation of working-class women in paid prostitution in the *Communist Manifesto* of 1848. Again, nearly forty years later, in *The Origin of the Family, Private Property and the State*, Engels (1972) wrote: 'Have we not seen that in the modern world monogamy and prostitution are indeed contradictions, but inseparable contradictions, poles of the same state of society?' (p. 139).

Victorian middle-class feminists spearheaded the campaigns against exploitation and persecution of prostitutes which they saw resulting from state regulation of prostitution, as part of a general attack on aggressive male sexuality and the double standard. Unlike moral reformers, with whom they found themselves allied, most of them saw quite clearly the connection between prostitution and the constraints placed on women's social and economic activity; low wages and not 'working-class immorality' were forcing women to take to the streets. The campaigns led by Josephine Butler and others in Britain against the Contagious Diseases Acts which required the registration of prostitutes represented a challenge to 'male centers of power such as the police, Parliament, and the medical and military establishments' (Walkowitz, 1980, p. 125). Feminists sought protection from male 'lust,' from repeated undesired pregnancies and from venereal disease, the scourge of the nineteenth century, through the adoption by men of 'female purity.' Christabel Pankhurst, the militant daughter of the often-imprisoned Mrs Emmeline Pankhurst, believed that men opposed the vote because they wanted to protect prostitution and the abuse of women. 'Votes for Women and Chastity for Men' was her slogan in 1913 (Weeks, 1981).

The question of the place of female sexuality and male power in the larger social context, and the ubiquitous, multivalent character of male violence against women could hardly have become a public issue twenty years ago. Until the 1960s what went on in the sanctity of the home was considered to be nobody's business, and if a woman was harassed outside her home it was probably because she deserved it. This attitude is still prevalent, but some dents have been made. Today sexual harassment of female employees of the United Nations can be openly discussed; the committee on human rights of the European Parliament can call on the Common Market countries to recognize that 'Europe is a field of action for pimping networks' and that an extensive traffic in women is taking place; the Swedish government can consider legislation that would punish rape regardless of the relationship between the persons involved (i.e., would recognize intercourse forced on a wife by a husband as an offense). These developments can be traced to the action of small groups of feminists who saw the connection between the way women are treated sexually and the way they are devalued socially and economically, and insisted that 'the personal is political.'

Second-wave femininists who had just begun to realize the extent of discrimination against women actually got this part of their education in feminism from men on the political left. Women who took part in the civil rights movement and the anti-war movement of the 1960s in the US soon discovered that Stokeley Carmichael, the black leader, spoke for the male sex when he said that the only position for a woman in the movement was prone. This, of course, after she made the coffee, typed the leaflets and stuffed the envelopes. Shulamith Firestone (1971) described it all in her inimitable style:

> In the sixties the boys split. They went to college and Down South. They traveled to Europe in droves. Some joined the Peace Corps; others went underground. But wherever they went they brought their camp followers. Liberated men needed groovy chicks who could swing with their new life style: women tried. They needed sex: women complied. But that's all they needed from women. . . . Wherever they went, whether Greenwich Village c. 1960, Berkeley or Mississippi c. 1964, Haight-Ashbury or the East Village c. 1967, they were still only 'chicks,' invisible as people. (p. 28)

Ellen Willis of the *Village Voice* recalls the anti-inaugural demonstration against President Richard Nixon in Washington in 1969 at which a woman speaker tried to add male chauvinism to the issues of war and racism:

> This isn't the protest against movement men . . . just fairly innocuous radical rhetoric – except that it's a good looking woman talking about women. The men go crazy. 'Take it off!' 'Take her off the stage and fuck her!' They yell and boo and guffaw at unwitting *double-entendres* like 'We must

take to the streets. . . .' If radical men can be so easily provoked into acting like rednecks (a Woman's Liberation group at the University of North Carolina was urinated on by male hecklers at a demonstration) what can we expect from others? (quoted in Mitchell, 1971, p. 85)

What could be expected from others has been recorded in hundreds of incidents, like the story of the sole female student in a pathology class at an upstate New York university who was assigned to work alone on a female corpse while her male colleagues worked in pairs on male corpses. Coming in early one morning she found a penis stuck in the vagina of her corpse. Typical medical student humor, perhaps? Exactly. Fortunately she had sufficient humor herself to hold up the offending penis in front of the class and ask: 'Did anybody lose this?' (Adams, 1983).

Alix Kates Shulman (1980) recalls from her own experience how feminists who felt victimized by the 'sexual revolution' began to make the degradation of women as dehumanized sex objects political. At the demonstration of sixty feminists against the Miss America Pageant in 1968, when the women filled a trash can with bras, girdles, curlers and spike-heeled shoes, the bra-burning myth was launched by the media and, in spite of its inaccuracy and spiteful intent, put radical feminism on the map. The radical feminists went on to apply their perception that sexuality is about power to abortion, rape, contraception, health, education, housework and motherhood. This consciousness spread to the rest of the woman's movement and influenced those women who were not prepared to make sexuality a central issue.

Most fundamental was the effect on socialist feminists who, on the basis of their own experience in male-dominated labor unions and left organizations, and in the light of new knowledge about the situation of women in the Soviet Union and other Eastern European countries, were rejecting the orthodox Marxist premise that all the oppression of women could be traced to private ownership of the means of production. Unwilling to accept transfer of the struggle entirely to the realm of ideas, they sought to extend the material causes to include aspects of sexuality (Hartmann, 1981b; Mackintosh, 1981; Mitchell, 1971). Angela Miles (1981) writes:

> Marxist and socialist feminists . . . [have] come to recognize the separateness of class and sexual domination and the importance of reproduction both to capitalism and to patriarchy. . . . This has opened the way for these feminists to insist on the necessity of developing a feminist theory and practise which integrates: feminism and Marxism, production and reproduction, and the social and psychological. (p. 490)

It is little more than a decade since Kate Millett (1970) and Germaine Greer (1971) kicked over the traces of the Eternal Feminine to expose in our literature and our practice – as Millett (1970) put it – 'the disgust, the contempt, the hostility, the violence, and the sense of filth with which our culture, or more specifically, its masculine sensibility, surrounds sexuality' – and with it women (p. 295). Since then feminism has experienced a backlash, and male violence against women has not diminished, but we have learned something about the role of sexuality in maintaining patriarchy, and the subject has been brought out into the open.

Shelters and hotlines for battered women have become part of social policy in many countries. 'Violence against women,' writes Allan Griswold Johnson (1980), 'is not part of the behavior of the lunatic fringe but emerges from the everyday fabric of relations between men and women in patriarchal society' (p. 137). He is talking specifically about the US. One thing Israeli women have discovered because they come from so many different parts of the world, Marcia Freedman, founder of the Israeli feminist movement and a member of the Knesset, told Geraldine Stern (1979), is that the situation of women is everywhere basically the same. In Israel:

> Battered wives are battered by men who are rabbis, who are policemen, who are generals in the army, who are doctors, lawyers, and who are perfectly sane but who are violent, and whose violence is not permitted in any other

sphere in the society, under penalty of law and punishment. But it is permitted in the home because of the very old attitude that the wife is the property of the husband and his home is his castle in which he may do as he likes. (p. 50)

The extent of rape and its nature as an instrument of power rather than an expression of uncontrollable male lust is now widely recognized, thanks to Susan Brownmiller (1976) and other authors. According to Johnson's 'conservative estimate,' 20–30 per cent of American females now 12 years old will experience a violent sexual attack some time in their lives, and this excludes the possibility of violence within marriage.

Rape is a widely used mechanism of social control, a way of putting woman in her place. According to Lotika Sarkar, a professor of law at the University of New Delhi, 90 per cent of rape in India is either committed by policemen or takes place in protective institutions (*Worldpaper*, July/August 1980). Gang rape represents a contempt for and a dehumanization of women so profound as to lead the perpetrators to regard their behavior as socially sanctioned. And indeed the four men who raped a woman in a bar in New Bedford, Massachusetts, on 6 March 1983, had every reason to think so since other customers egged them on and the owner did not notify the authorities. The rapists were still in the bar when the victim returned with the police and identified them. The community responded to the guilty verdict with a protest march. It was the victim who had to leave town (Boston *Globe*, 24 March 1984).

Misogyny pervades our history and our culture. Major religious traditions – Judeo-Christian, Muslim and Hindu – have preached both women's inferiority to men and their connection with evil, sin, danger and pollution. Male domination, prescribed by Judaism, became part of Christian theology. 'You are the devil's gateway. . . . How easily you destroyed man, the image of God. Because of the death which you brought upon us, even the Son of God had to die.' Mary Daly (1973), who quotes these words of Tertullian, a third-century Roman defender of the faith (p. 44), reminds us of similarly accusatory statements by Thomas Aquinas, Martin Luther, John Knox and others. She points out that the 'good' image of Mary did not rehabilitate women since she was an inimitable role model, having been conceived without sin. If the Protestant bourgeoisie found it convenient to proclaim woman the angel in the house (Janeway, 1980), it was to inveigh with increased vigor against the temptress outside the home. Hindu and Muslim ideologies reflect fear of the mystical power women appear to exercise over men's lives and potency, and have dealt with this threat with forced marriage, segregation and seclusion (Al-Hibri, 1982; El Saadawi, 1982; Wadley, 1977).

Some of the worst practices stemming from religious beliefs have been abandoned or at least modified: the burning of witches, the punishment of adultery by death or public humiliation, prohibitions on birth control and divorce, suttee (the burning of widows), purdah (the seclusion of women). One brutal practice which survives in a belt of states in equatorial Africa is genital mutilation – ranging from clipping of the clitoris in young girls to infibulation: the removal of the clitoris and the sewing together of the vulva to form a barrier to intercourse. As African feminists point out, Islam does not actually prescribe female circumcision. So deeply is it embedded in some patriarchal societies, however, that efforts to change the practice are regarded by both women and men as violations of sacred custom (Hosken, 1979; Kneerim and Shur, n.d.).

Some brutal practices have reappeared under the pressure of economic conditions. In recent years an epidemic of 'dowry deaths' has swept India: brides are burned by husbands and in-laws when the husband fails to extort additional dowry payments from his wife's family after the marriage. Although dowry is illegal in India, authorities are unable or unwilling to act. In rural China the official limitation on family size to one child has led some parents to make sure that the one child is a boy. Female infanticide is practised because a son is still perceived as necessary insurance against poverty in old age.

Marriage, legally and socially enforced as the only institution through which women can experience love and achieve status and economic security, has been analyzed by Adrienne Rich (1980) as a pervasive instrument of male power. By arguing the 'innate' sexual orientation of women toward men and classifying love between women as a perversion, men have enforced their right of physical, emotional and economic access to women. But if what men and women 'are' is socially constructed, if meaning is given to biological sex by society, then an erotic relationship between men and women is not pre-ordained as part of a Grand Design on the part of Nature to perpetuate the species. In fact, for most of history, marriage had nothing to do with erotic attraction.

If heterosexual attraction was innate, it would not have been necessary to use laws, religion and social ostracism to enforce it. The issue is not, as Rich writes, good marriages versus bad ones, but compulsory heterosexuality, the absence of choice. Women have had nowhere else to go for economic security or personal identity; the alternative was – still is, in most societies – to become a marginal member of the community. For Rich this is the central factor in women's oppression in our western culture.

It was Simone De Beauvoir (1971) in *The Second Sex*, first published in France in 1949, who introduced most of us to the concept of Woman the Other. De Beauvoir traced Otherness as a fundamental category of human thought. There is, she said, in consciousness itself a fundamental hostility to every other consciousness. This sense of Otherness was not originally attached to the female sex but was transferred to women, together with a sense of male superiority, in the course of prehistory when men grasped unconsciously the 'transcendental,' 'cultural,' character of their work (hunting, warfare), involving control over nature, as opposed to women's reproductive work which is rooted in nature and merely repetitive, or 'immanent.' Woman's acceptance of her own devaluation, de Beauvoir said, results from her acceptance of the cultural argument.

Yet biology is not destiny, she insists, and woman can consciously choose transcendence. Indeed de Beauvoir believes she will. '[There] is no reason to conclude that her ovaries condemn her to live for ever on her knees' (p. 727).

The common humanity of human beings is more important than the differences that distinguish them.

De Beauvoir provided a breathtaking excursion into their own lives for a generation of feminists, but there are problems with her definition of Otherness as a fundamental category of human thought. De Beauvoir believes that certain historical conditions will enable woman to liberate herself – participation in production and freedom from reproduction. But, as Mary Lowenthal Feldstiner points out (1980), either the sense of Otherness is part of human consciousness and cannot be erased or it isn't. If it is not an immutable part of our thinking process and can be overcome by women's will to transcendence, then it is not that prehistoric source of domination that de Beauvoir describes. This remains an unresolved contradiction.

Other aspects of de Beauvoir's argument have been superseded by new knowledge. As we have seen, women in all probability shared with men from earliest times that 'transcendent' control over nature. Further, anthropologists now cast doubt on the assertion put forward by de Beauvoir, Sherry B. Ortner (1974), and other authors that all societies make Western-type distinctions between culture and nature, that they consider culture an instrument for suppressing nature, and that they associate men with the first and women with the second.

L. J. Jordanova, in a collection of articles edited by MacCormack and Strathern (1980), contributes a much-needed reminder that our present notions of nature and culture, and the connections we make between them and femaleness or maleness, are not eternal but date from the eighteenth century. Moreover, the use de Beauvoir, Ortner and others make of them divest these ideas of their original complexity.

Marilyn Strathern, in this same collection, makes clear that our own Western thought does not give one single, unambiguous meaning to nature or culture. She suggests some of the contradictions:

When thinking of culture as common to the species we may refer to it as a manifestation of 'human nature': when thinking of it as particularizing mankind in relation to the rest of the world we envisage culture as an ingredient adding refinement to a given 'animal nature' we share with other species. . . . At one point culture is a creative, active force which produces form and structure out of a passive, given nature. At another, culture is the end product of a process, tamed and refined, and dependent for energy upon resources outside itself. (p. 178)

Two major pitfalls await the author of a psychological explanation for male dominance. One is the temptation to root it in prehistory by giving modern psychological concepts an eternal validity. The other is the urge to stand economic determinism on its head: instead of locating the source of ideas entirely in economic development, economic events are the direct product of preexisting ideas.

Juliet Mitchell (1975) in her *Psychoanalysis and Feminism* paved the way for a reconsideration of Freud by the women's movement which had initially rejected what it saw as his 'anatomy is destiny' approach to the female personality. Attempting to synthesize Freud and Marx, she rejected both biological determinism and solutions to women's oppression that rely entirely on struggles against social institutions and sexist attitudes.

Mitchell stressed the need for a theory which provides a structural analysis of the ways in which ideology and the cultural construction of sexuality are rooted not only within our consciousness . . . but crucially within our unconscious. (McDonough and Harrison, 1978, pp. 18–19)

In Mitchell's reading, Freud did not justify patriarchy, he analyzed it. Interpreting Freud and Claude Lévi-Strauss, she regards patriarchy as transhistorical, specific to all civilizations, synonymous with human culture, because it was a social necessity. In Lévi-Strauss's understanding of anthropological data, the incest taboo was the inevitable cultural law that made it possible for society to survive and develop, through rules that required marriage to take place outside the original kinship unit. This was universally enforced through the exchange of women by men (a process to be understood symbolically rather than literally). Mitchell reads the oedipus complex – the triangular relationship between the child and its parents – as a metaphor for the ways people have internalized, in various societies, this cultural imperative: the incest taboo and the law of the father.

She argues that although patriarchy and the oedipal crisis are both part of humanity's entry into society, their concrete expression takes different forms under different modes of production. This allows her to predict the end of patriarchy, since under advanced capitalism the kinship system, now the nuclear family, has become irrelevant and has been replaced in importance by class structures.

Although it was Mitchell's intention to construct a materialist theory of the way the male and female personalities are formed, her account presents a problem similar to that posed by de Beauvoir. It follows from her argument that patriarchy is coterminous with human nature in the sense that human society cannot come into being without it; the conditions for its acceptance already exist in the structure of the unconscious (otherwise women could just as well exchange men, but, says Lévi-Strauss, they don't). This implies that there is some distilled essence of patriarchy that existed before any of its concrete manifestations, a pre-designed structure of human relations into which humanity has been locked since an unspecified point in prehistory. Yet this abstraction is now ready to be overthrown in a concrete, historically determined situation. But, if we place any value on consistency, we must conclude as in the case of de Beauvoir's 'Otherness' that if patriarchy is an ahistorical abstraction built into the unconscious mind it cannot be exorcized by concrete social struggle. Either it is an eternal quality of thought existing independent of historical conditions or it isn't.

Azizah Al-Hibri (1981), on the other hand, attributes to prehistoric man the *conscious* collective intention to suppress womankind. In her argument, man experienced the female Other as 'a substantial ego threat' (p. 172) before the dawn of history because he realized that woman, through her mysterious biological processes of reproduction, held the key to immortality. Man therefore seized upon production (technology) to compensate for his perceived inferiority and as a means to the domination of women.

The achievement of immortality by controlling nature, and thus dominating women's powers as part of nature: this idea becomes the moving force of history in Al-Hibri's account. It would hardly have been acceptable for man, she writes, if woman reproduced and also produced. Hence, to preserve the fragile male ego, woman was excluded from production. As history progressed, she argues, dominant male ideologies were not directed just against women but also called for the oppression of a majority of male Others. Technology and patriarchy served each other, producing feudalism, colonialism, capitalism and imperialism.

This version of history, which purports to show that capitalism is an advanced stage of an ahistorical, psychologically determined patriarchy, presents us with a new set of assumptions. An innate need to overcome feelings of inadequacy crowds out the primary human needs of food and shelter as stimuli to conscious activity. Environment, warfare, territorial expansion, discovery, invention, do not interact to change human thinking; they are all products of a single male idea and simply reinforce it. Women disappear as active agents. A 'conspiracy theory' that attributes to male thought such singleness of purpose and consistency flies in the face of historical evidence. Once again we are faced with the eternal woman-nature/man-culture split discussed above. Al-Hibri also pushes back into the dawn of history numerous other relatively modern concepts – not only longings for personal immortality and conceptualized feelings of envy and alienation, but interpretive tools of psychoanalysis such as frustration and ego threat.

A concept frequently advanced to explain the male will to dominate is that of womb envy, introduced into psychoanalysis by Karen Horney (1926) more than half a century ago. Horney identified in her male patients a strong unconscious envy of women's ability to bear children, and she suggested that this could have been the powerful driving force impelling men to establish their superiority and the supremacy of their values. Evidence that womb envy and fear

of women's powers are universal, primal experiences has
been found by Bruno Bettelheim, Ashley Montagu and others
in tribal initiation rites such as circumcision, ritual homo-
sexuality, the acting out of childbirth by men, and in rules of
avoidance such as the segregation of women during menstruation (Hage, 1981).

These interpretations have been strongly challenged by
many anthropologists, who insist that tribal rituals have
been misinterpreted by observers who impose meanings on
them from alien cultures. They want these rites looked at not
as isolated events but as part of each society's totality of
beliefs and ceremonies.

One of this last group, Per Hage (1981), looks at the
actual meaning given boys' initiation rites, such as induced
bleeding by penile incision and ritual homosexual acts, in
New Guinea. He holds, in agreement with other authors, that
rather than making men into pseudo-women they make men
into men.

> The relation between these rites and female physiology
> is based not on envy or identity but on analogy, that
> is, a perceived connexion between the onset of
> menstruation and growth, or on generalisation. . . . If
> [semen] induces growth in the foetus then it may also be
> thought to induce growth subsequently at adolescence. . . .
> They are magical acts which make a man more like a
> man. . . . (p. 272)

Taboos surrounding women are not necessarily evidence
that men fear contamination. In Marla Powers's (1980)
research the segregation of women during menstruation by
Muskogee Indians from Oklahoma is necessary because the
powers of men and women are so different that they must be
kept separate. As one Muskogee told her, 'Men must take a
sweat bath once a month, while women are purifying themselves to keep their medicine effective.' Many American
Indian tribes believe that men have a limited amount of
semen, and proscribe intercourse with a menstruating
women so that it will not be wasted. Powers hopes that 'we
may learn to desensitize ourselves from Western negative
notions of female physiology and address ourselves to the

need to make a *unified* analysis of women's symbolic and material lives' (p. 65).

To give another example Elizabeth Faithorn (1975) writes of the Eastern Highlands of New Guinea, and especially of the Káfe group whom she has studied, that both men and women have the capacity to endanger others. Menstrual blood and male semen are, when properly channelled, regarded as powerful forces in society. When improperly controlled they can cause death. The fact that only women have been recognized as polluters, and that pollution is seen to threaten males only is 'related to the generally perfunctory and negative ways in which Highland women are depicted in the ethnographic literature' (p. 130). Káfe women do not consider themselves inferior, and Káfe men consider women strong and important to the functioning of society.

In the search for psychological reasons for men's insistence on superiority, exceptional interest has been attracted by the work of two writers, Dorothy Dinnerstein (*The Mermaid and the Minotaur*, 1977) and Nancy Chodorow (*The Reproduction of Mothering*, 1978). They make use of 'object relations' theory, a development within psychoanalytic theory, to explain not the origins of male dominance and the exclusion of women from public life but their staying power. Employing somewhat different arguments, both hold that it is the female monopoly of mothering that perpetuates our prevalent 'human malaise' – the 'hate, fear, loathing, contempt, and greed' that Dinnerstein finds pervading the very atmosphere we breathe (p. 88). Both believe the cycle can be broken only by equal participation by fathers in child care.

While denying that humans are born with a biologically programmed sex drive and accepting that the meaning of sexuality is socially given, both propose to explain how sexuality plays a role of central significance in the development of personality, how the external world is internalized not just at the level of conscious reason but in the very creation of the subjective self. Because they claim to penetrate the depths of the unconscious these explanations seem more convincing than theories of conscious sex-role learning and appear to explain why efforts to counter sex-role stereotyping have had such meagre results. They also hold out concrete possibilities for change.

Angela Miles (1981) writes:

These analyses help integrative feminists acknowledge and explore the current deep and disturbing differences between men and women that they have sensed go well beyond mere sex role training, and at the same time to assert the ultimate possibility of a non-alienated and human world for all. . . . [p. 492] [This development] has . . . opened the way for non-reductionist socialist, Marxist, cultural, lesbian, and radical feminist concern with reproduction to become the beginnings of the integrated analysis of social/personal, public/private institutions and experience that the more sophisticated thinkers of other radical movements have also been seeking. [p. 491]

Both Dinnerstein and Chodorow make use of Freud's observation that female and male personality is importantly shaped by the fact that girls, unlike boys, are raised by someone of the same sex in infancy. For Dinnerstein it is fear of overwhelming female power inculcated in the infant wholly dependent on its mother that drives both men and women to accept male authority. For Chodorow it is the less secure gender identity of boys as a result of having been raised by a parent of the opposite sex that produces the male need to dominate women.

Dinnerstein argues that because in our society the roles of men and women are so distinct, the female child need never resolve her inevitable feelings of ambivalence and dependence toward her mother. Girls continue to experience the mother as all-powerful, and because they potentially share this power they accept men's power in public life. At the same time the girl solves her ambivalent feelings toward her mother by transferring her positive feelings to her father. A boy, in contrast, can identify with his father and with the outside world only at the price of learning to keep his feelings for his original love, his mother, under control. Our asymmetrical parenting arrangements thus foster 'complementary forms of childishness' in adults (p. 88). Early rage at the first parent is used by the boy to consolidate his ties with his own sex by establishing a disdainful distance from women, while the girl loosens her tie with her own sex by establishing a worshipful dependent relationship toward men.

In Chodorow's version the fact that boys are forced to give up their sense of primary identification with the mother in order to achieve masculine identity, and the more abstract and impersonal figure of the often-absent father, produce a male personality unsuited to caring roles, but especially fitted to the demands of the capitalist labor market. Mothers maintain the sense of oneness with their daughters for a long time, and women come to need this relationship of mergence and dependence. Since men cannot supply it, women seek fulfilment in having children of their own. Thus mothering perpetuates itself, and female parenting fits both sexes for their conventional rules in a segregated world. Like Dinner-stein, Chodorow projects the influence of this parenting beyond personal relationships to our most pressing social ills, with which she sees us as too emotionally crippled to deal.

A basic question that is inevitably raised about psycho-analytical accounts of behavior is whether one can in principle, and if so under what circumstances, deduce from unconsciously registered events and emotions, reconstructed in clinical cases, firm generalizations about why the rest of the population acts as it does and what it would do under other conditions. Freud himself did not make such predictive claims for his science (Elshtain, 1983; Person, 1980; Wilson, 1981).

For those who accept these accounts of personality development there are still inconsistencies. These 'bad arrangements,' it seems, nevertheless produce good qualities in women which men are asked to emulate. Men are unfit to parent by reason of their upbringing; yet they are to take up parenting to the benefit of everyone.

Beyond these objections there is the basic problem: whether, as Jean Bethke Elshtain (1983) asks, these theories can bear the explanatory weight placed upon them. Can this one-sided parenting account for all the manifestations of sexual inequality? Can the misuse of male power to violate nature and exploit others really be explained, as in

Dinnerstein's account, by the male's 'early rage' against his mother? Or, with Chodorow, by the fact that mothering produces men appropriate to the capitalist world? In this model, says Elshtain, 'cultures ... are shrunk down to a single point of order and drained of their inner meaning' (p. 5).

If the infantile experience is so powerful, what accounts for the many women for whom mothering is fraught with conflict (Sayers, 1982)? What explains the difficulty women have in accepting their role (a common problem for psycho-analysis) (Wilson, 1981); the organized resistance to exploit-ation; the men who do not fit the 'masculine' pattern, and all the other deviations from the model supposedly produced by mothering? If, as both authors acknowledge, this opposition exists, what is the evidence that conscious effort to transcend infantile experience is not stronger than early unconscious experience?

The responsive chord both these authors strike is elicited by the vivid and recognizable landscape they paint of pre-valent contemporary relationships and attitudes. The solution − to involve men in parenting − is one that has already been proposed by feminists as a way to lighten women's double burden. The arguments put forward by these authors make it a 'progressive demand for the integration of men into valuable important relationships in a way that would have large, personal, political and social consequences' (Miles, 1981, p. 492).

The theoretical question raised by critics of Dinnerstein and Chodorow is not, however, whether involvement of men in child care is important, but whether parenting arrange-ments are really the kingpin that holds together the whole patriarchal structure. Would pulling out this one pin bring down the house, reinforced as it is by laws and institutions? Is it, in fact, possible to bring about symmetrical parenting without first modifying the supporting institutions?

This question becomes especially pertinent in view of the increasing number of women bringing up children alone. The issue becomes not just how to involve fathers with their own children, but how to incorporate men into the whole process of childrearing. Clearly, some general social changes will have to precede a change in child-care patterns, before a change in parenting can affect our social system. We are back to confronting political realities.

Obviously a short account cannot do justice to the arguments for or against the theories I have mentioned here. It should be plain, however, that the search for psychological explanations of male dominance is still in its early stages. The tendency at present is to isolate a single promising factor from what appears to be an infinitely tangled web and make it shoulder the blame: conscious or unconscious envy and fear of women's procreative powers and the need to control them; desire for unlimited access to women through enforced heterosexuality; personality distortion resulting from female monopoly of parenting. We are a long way from a synthesis or from bridges that will link psychological explanations to theories rooted in historical development in a satisfactory way.

All the examples given in this chapter illustrate the difficulties of constructing a universal psychological explanation of the male will to dominate that will be valid for all cultures. All the theories purporting to describe the mechanism by which sexuality is transformed into power are anchored in our modern Western understanding of the meaning of sexuality, and they depend for their validity on a variety of current assumptions, whose life may be short and which are in some cases mutually exclusive. For example, it is virtually impossible to hold that heterosexual marriage is an instrument of oppression (or even that families based on heterosexual unions are only one of several normal lifestyles) and to insist on the necessity of a close infant–father relationship for society's health. The latter theory makes of woman-headed families and lesbian households with children a threat to progress.

Eighteenth-century scientific theory gave us woman allied with nature through her biology and, like nature, destined for domination by man. Theology, medicine and educational theory all found supporting objective proofs for this. Nineteenth-century anthropology gave us Man the Hunter, based on male brain and brawn. Patriarchy could now be traced back to the primeval forests. Twentieth-century history gave us the woman whose place had always been in the home. All these widely accepted propositions have had to give way before new evidence or old evidence that had gone unnoticed. Twenty-five years ago it would not have been possible to identify the female monopoly of parenting as the root cause of the major problems of society because the 'scientific evidence' of the time pointed to the child's primary and continuing need for constant maternal care. One could say that the idea of shared parenting was not at that time available as a resource for theory building.

The feminist research explosion of the past decade has made us conscious of the enormous historical and cultural diversity in relationships between men and women which can only be imperfectly described by any one discipline. In the light of our experience with the way 'truths' can change, we are sceptical of all 'final answers.' We are more aware of the shifting sand under the scientific statements and taken-for-granted concepts on which policy recommendations are based.

Chapter 8

THE TYRANNY OF ECONOMICS

I believe that the discipline of economics is not viable. It obscures the way people in industrial cultures talk to each other about *what is valuable* under drastically changed conditions. (Hazel Henderson, *The Politics of the Solar Age*, 1981, p. 8)

The personal is not just political. It is also economic.

The source of women's special susceptibility to poverty lies in the fact that much of what is defined as 'women's work' takes place outside the boundary of the world's economy as men see it, and therefore has no value in the economic sense. Since there is no yardstick other than price for measuring value, women's work remains invisible out there in the 'real world.'

This was not true until industrialization gradually took work out of the home and created commodities, goods which were not exchanged or sold directly by those who made them but were produced for a third person who sold them at a profit. In preindustrial capitalism women still contributed substantially to the support of the household by working for the market as well as producing for the family, so that the magnitude of women's contribution was plain. In the US, household manufacture and family farm agriculture were still important in the first decades of the twentieth century (Brownlee, 1979).

In tribal societies where everyone works and everyone eats and property belongs to the community, questions of value do not arise. At some point in prehistory the division of labor developed to the point where private exchanges occurred. We do not know much about how baskets may have been exchanged for axes or pottery for hides: presumably values varied from transaction to transaction. Much exchange probably took the form of gifts of symbolic value, as is still the case in contemporary preindustrial societies.

When barter became inconvenient money arose, and with it the problem of how to measure exchange value, a puzzle that occupied Aristotle. He understood that goods had to be comparable to be exchanged, but he concluded that this comparable quality was absolute, something intrinsic to the goods. In European feudal society land was the only source of wealth and, since early feudal estates were subsistence economies, the collection and redistribution of produce was more important than money. With the rise of mercantile capitalism in the sixteenth century came the theory that national wealth depended on having a favorable balance of trade. Governments chartered trading companies to sell domestic products abroad, raised tariffs on foreign goods, forbade the export of gold and silver, subsidized shipping companies and controlled their dealings. No real theory of value was developed until the concentration of manufacture in factories in the eighteenth century made it necessary to explain the economic activities of 'men' in production, to show how prices came to include profit, and ultimately to justify profit (Hay, 1965; Meek, 1967; Roll, 1939).

Today's economic theory lets the market decide what is valuable. Only paid labor produces value; this is the ideology of the gender division of labor. There is no reason why we have to accept this definition of value. It is no more eternally valid or scientific than the conventionally used concepts of poverty, class, work and progress that we are learning to question because they define women in terms of men. As we have seen, using these labels women's poverty is disguised, their class is ambiguous, 'their' work is unpaid, and the benefits of progress, defined as technological advance, tend to pass them by.

We are intimidated by the pretensions of Western economics, as it is practised in the universities and by governments, to be an objective scientific discipline dealing with the basics of life. This claim has, however, come under attack with increasing vehemence by ranking members of the profession itself. The most obvious example of fallibility since World War II has been the collapse of the 'trickle-down' theory, according to which sheer economic growth produces jobs and eventually wipes out poverty at the bottom of the ladder; on an international scale the same development model is supposed to trickle benefits down from the First World to the Third, and within poor countries to the poorest people. It just doesn't work that way, as we have seen in earlier chapters. Peru exports fish protein to the US as cattle feed, while the US distributes protein-fortified soft drinks in Peru. Production and trade increase, but so do unemployment and hunger.

The suspicion that economics as currently practised is some kind of a word game has trickled down to a large number of people in Western countries in the wake of repeated announcements that the 'deepest recession since World War II' was over and that in the US, at least, the growth rate of the GNP had returned to normal. If recovery is consistent with 35 million unemployed in the industrially advanced Western countries, with millions hungry and homeless in the US alone, then we can all say with Humpty Dumpty that 'a word means just what I choose it to mean.'

This is not to deny that there is a place for economics that tracks or attempts to predict the movement of goods, prices, money and labor on the market or within firms. It is the arrogant conflation of market values with all values, and the pretence of economics to be objective because it deals with hard cold numbers, that exasperates many professionals of diverse views within the discipline. Thomas Balogh, Kenneth Boulding, John Kenneth Galbraith, Robert Heilbroner, Gunnar Myrdal, Joan Robinson, E. F. Schumacher and Barbara Ward are some of the better known names. The trend to self-criticism is documented by Hazel Henderson, ecologist and futurist, in her two books, *Creating Alternative Futures* (1978) and *The Politics of the Solar Age* (1981). In the latter she writes:

> The crux of the crisis of economics of all schools of thought is that they all share the same hypnotism of money, looking only at those sectors of production and

consumption in their countries that are monetized and involve cash transactions. This colossal error of equating the monetized half of most industrial countries with the whole system of production, consumption and maintenance is common to all branches of economics and accounts for its one-dimensional, linear, partial view, as opposed to the wider realities of seeing economies whole. (p. 25)

The ecological movement has provided the impetus for one aspect of the debate over the viability of conventional economics. Although 'realists' have questioned various doomsday predictions setting actual dates for the exhaustion of raw material resources vital to industrial growth, the public has gradually taken hold of the idea that it is not a matter of whether we have enough oil, coal, copper, iron or other minerals to last twenty-five, fifty or two hundred years. The point is that these and other natural resources are non-replaceable. They cannot be exploited indefinitely, as has been assumed in all existing economic models.

John Kenneth Galbraith, in his *The Affluent Society* (1958), questioned the sense of relying on 'market forces' that put plastic junk on the market, producing air and water pollution as a side effect. Kenneth Boulding, a former president of the American Economic Association, dubbed this habit of treating natural resources as a limitless frontier 'cowboy economics' (Henderson, 1978, p. 66). E. F. Schumacher provided what was probably the most influential critique of economics' bookkeeping methods – the custom of treating fossil fuels and living nature as income instead of as part of the total capital we are using, and by far the larger part at that. 'If we treated them as capital items,' he writes in *Small is Beautiful* (1973), 'we should be concerned with conservation; we should do everything in our power to try and minimize their current rate of use' (p. 15). 'It is inherent in the methodology of economics *to ignore man's dependence on the natural world*' (p. 44). Economics, he says, should distinguish between those manufactured goods made from renewable resources and those based on non-renewable resources. 'Cost' to a manufacturer is the same whether he uses up five dollars' worth of oil or five dollars' worth of coconuts, and his decision will be 'rational' if he makes the choice that brings the greatest profit. To the rest of us the two costs are not the same, however, since oil supplies cannot be renewed. Their over-exploitation should be counted as disruptive growth.

Many critics have been pointing out for some time that in addition to ignoring the drain on resources, the GNP takes no notice of the social costs of industrial growth. Money spent on cleaning up pollution and waste, on building health facilities to treat occupational diseases, traffic injuries and stress, legal services that attempt to unravel the litigation arising from the negative effects of growth, and finally the billions poured into armaments – all these expenditures are considered part of the national wealth. Many of the social costs are born by the informal, non-monetary sector of the economy – by families and voluntary charitable work. Both the UN and the OECD have responded to this criticism with projects to develop internationally comparable indicators of the 'quality of life.' These attempt to quantify such social concerns as health, housing, employment, work environment, personal safety and social opportunity. It is unlikely, however, that quality of life measurements will be substituted for the GNP in national or international bookkeeping as long as this bookkeeping is done wholly in terms of monetary transactions. Nevertheless, they help to create the realization that this sum of monetary transactions is not a measure of real wealth and certainly not of welfare. 'The bottom line' does not tell us how real people live, much less what is happening to their lives.

The awareness that our environment is finite and that what we are measuring with the GNP is not real wealth or welfare has underlined the whole question of the validity of growth as a measure of economic health. How can we go on expanding if the natural world that supplies the raw materials is limited? At present 20–30 per cent of the world's population uses 80 per cent of the natural resources consumed. It is impossible to imagine industrial development in the Third World without realizing that a decrease in total incomes, investment, production and consumption as presently defined will have to occur in the most advanced countries. Western-style growth was a once-only historical phenomenon, and countries now industrializing will not be able to repeat it. It has given birth to processes we can no longer control. We have to question our old assumptions and start thinking about how to live in industrial society in a completely new way.

Neither can we depend on the Technological Fix to keep the cornucopia flowing. The computer will *not* bring us all in to a happy landing, as Mary B. Anderson (1983) points out. She reminds us that technologies are not value-free or value-neutral, that they tend to replicate the society that developed them because they frequently determine beforehand not only how we solve a problem but what we consider the problem to be. Consider the simple fact that we can put a woman into space and that we are prepared to deliver a missile to Moscow in a matter of minutes, while African women have to walk an hour or more a day just to keep their families supplied with water. The space-age technocrat is not programmed to recognize human priorities and solve the African water supply problem first.

Another piece of economic mythology that has come under attack is the idea that a country's economic health can be accurately and scientifically pictured by a mathematical model. Since its eighteenth-century beginnings, economics has had ambitions to rank as a science on a par with Newtonian physics.

> The triumph of Newtonian mechanics in the eighteenth and nineteenth centuries established physics as the prototype of a 'hard' science against which all other sciences were measured. The closer scientists could come to emulating the methods of physics, and the more of its concepts they were able to use, the higher the standing of their discipline in the scientific community. (Capra, 1982, p. 188)

Surely, the analysts of human society argued, economic systems, like the systems of nature, were subject to universal laws based on objective phenomena that could be expressed mathematically. Economic textbooks today still operate with a 'core economics' that derives from Adam Smith, who held that the 'invisible hand' of the market guides everyone to use resources for the benefit of all. The idea that it is possible to discover laws governing human behavior on which it will be possible to build a universally valid science of economics dies hard.

It was a lost cause from the beginning, as the physicist Fritjof Capra (1982) points out. The subject matter of physics and biology is given, within limits, and their physical phenomena remain relatively stable over time, so that it is possible to express certain relationships in mathematical formulae. Economics, like other social sciences, deals with complex human behavior in continually changing social relationships and evolving environmental conditions. No set of equations can capture its dynamics. Scientific experiments must be replicable and theoretical calculations are tested by alternative procedures before they are accepted. 'These standards do not prevail in the social sciences and it seems vain to expect that they ever could,' writes Joan Robinson (1981, p. 92). She comments further that people are much more inclined to bend the evidence to fit their preconceived opinions when they are studying human society than when they are studying the external physical world where their own personal interests are not so obviously involved.

The triumph of the idea that the operation of market forces could be reduced to mathematics dates from the late nineteenth century when Thomas Jevons argued that 'utility,' and not labor, as the classical economists had held, determined value. While consumers' subjective desires could not actually be measured, 'utility,' or the quality in a thing that makes you want it, could be mathematically expressed by price through Jevons's 'Calculus of Pleasure and Pain' comparable to 'the Science of Statical Mechanics' (Dobb, 1973, p. 168). 'Marginal utility' is the price beyond which you are not prepared to go to buy some more of something. It thus purports to be a measure of demand.

This approach takes it as given that, under conditions of free competition, consumers naturally buy in such a way as to 'maximize' utility. It also assumes that labor, capital and land all appear on the market as independent 'factors' and make use of supply and demand to maximize their income. The entire economy is pictured as a mechanism with an inherent tendency to move toward a state of equilibrium in which each individual is doing the best for him/herself. Equilibrium is a concept borrowed from physics, however. There is no evidence that human society tends naturally toward equilibrium. What this 'marginal utility' theory says, as Meek (1967) points out, is that what is important is not the socio-economic relations between people, but the psychological relations between people and goods. It demonstrates the 'innate rationality' of competitive capitalism.

The present trend to mathematical economics and econometrics continues the same mechanistic approach in a global world where free competition does not exist, where monopolies set prices, labor unions bargain for wages, consumers make their choice after the fact, their demands are manipulated by advertising, and the pendulum swings from inflation to unemployment without passing through the state of equilibrium.

Gunnar Myrdal (1973) of Sweden, one of the world's best-known economists whom many of his colleagues would like to read out of the club because he corrupts economics with sociology (i.e., people), has denied throughout most of his long career that economics is or can be an exact science. Subjective valuations, he insists, enter into the research from start to finish, from the original concept to the variables chosen and the way the final results are presented. Moreover, the chances of constructing a valid mathematical model have diminished because of 'a shrinkage of the ordinary economist's training, interests and knowledge' since World War II: 'By knowing so little about the real world, and even about what other social sciences have found out about that world, he can live more undisturbed by doubts in his and his colleagues' model world' (p. 62). Not that econometric measurements cannot be useful, but the results will be no better than the data selected, he continues.

Economists use, for instance, a concept 'market,' which has no resemblance to a real market. And on the basis of this abstraction they carry out their analysis in terms of aggregates (like 'supply' and 'demand,' 'input' and 'output') or averages (like levels of 'wages' or 'incomes'). . . . Exactly what this type of abstraction means is not even attempting to dig deeper under the observable facts of human behavior, which are then dealt with in a very summary fashion. (pp. 141–2)

Economists, Myrdal says, explain away the irrelevance of their abstractions by insisting that they deal only with 'economic factors,' but the definition of economic factors involves the scrutiny of 'non-economic factors' as well. And there is no proof that the economic factors accounted for by aggregates and averages are always the relevant ones. 'The isolation of one part of social reality by demarcating it as "economic" is logically not feasible. In reality there are no "economic," "sociological," or "psychological" problems, but just problems, and they are all complex' (p 142).

Thomas Balogh (1982), a former minister of state in the British government, likewise attributes the irrelevance of much of 'fashionable economics' to the use of mathematical models, unsuited by their nature to express the kaleidoscopic character of economic events. He dismisses the 'rigor' of current conventional economic thought as rigor mortis.

The part of social reality that has received least attention from the critics of establishment economics is the debt the market owes the vast number of subsistence producers and homemakers, the non-paid pursuits that reproduce the working population and absorb many of the social costs of the world of hard cash. In spite of the studies that attribute values to housework that rival the total output of industrial goods, for economists the housewife is still just a consumer. Yet worldwide, the subsistence producers outnumber the wage workers.

Some of the bookkeeping anomalies collected by Newland (1979) illustrate the confusion of conventional economic concepts in the face of this reality. In Iran, of the many activities nomad women perform, including shearing and milking animals, hauling water, collecting firewood, making cheese and yoghurt, thread, clothing, tents and carpets, the only production that appears in national statistics is that of dairy products and woollen textiles. In the Republic of Congo, women's food processing is counted but not their handicrafts. Taiwan leaves out handicrafts but assigns a monetary value to water carrying and food gathering. But in Nigeria wood and water are considered free, so collecting them is not work.

Women's unpaid work has not fared any better in Marxist economics, although Marx did not consider himself an economist and fiercely rejected the premises and methodology of his mid-nineteenth-century contemporaries. Instead of beginning with the 'natural laws' of the market discerned by Adam Smith, he took as his field the whole of consciously directed productive activity that distinguishes humans from the rest of nature. With the development of tools, he observed, labor becomes a collective social process, and human beings act not only on nature but on one another; in changing nature they change themselves.

This was the clue, for Marx, to the movement of human history. His life study was not the circulation of inanimate things but the relationship of people in the productive process. The essential feature of capitalist production relations, whose operation it was his lifetime's work to illuminate, was that those who owned property were able to extract a profit from those who did not. Although they did not engage in any productive activity themselves, capitalists were able over time to accumulate wealth at the expense of the working class.

How had this system been imposed on workers to begin with? Marx drew a crucial distinction between labor and labor power. He argued that capitalism could not develop until a large part of the population had been deprived of all other sources of livelihood and was forced to sell its labor power – its capacity to produce – on the market. In other words, labor power had become a commodity and, like other commodities, sold at its value. Unlike other commodities, however, it had the power to create more than its own value.

As Marx expressed it, the value of commodities, and thus their price, will tend to be proportional to the average amount of labor normally used to produce them, expressed as 'socially necessary labor time.' The value of the commodity labor power then, its price, its wage, is represented by the socially necessary labor time required to reproduce the worker's capacity to work; in other words, to buy the worker's necessary wants. Since, in the course of the working day, the worker produces more than the value of the goods he consumes, this margin represents 'surplus value,' or the capitalist's profit. Profit is the difference between the value of labor power and the value of its product.

Needless to say, this is not a formula for working out how much the boss makes out of the individual worker. Marx's argument is that the labor force is paid the cost of the commodities it needs to live at its historically determined level of living, including its education and training and the support of children who will eventually replace the present workers, and that this sum is less than the value of the total product that the labor force produces.

This theory of surplus value is Marx's statement of the general nature of profits, the general socio-economic relations that exist among 'men' as commodity producers, as he expounded it in Volume I of *Capital*. It is based on a purely theoretical demonstration model of simple, competitive capitalist production, with no collective bargaining, in which profit depends only on labor and all commodities are assumed to sell at their value. It is not supposed to represent any particular historical period in the development of capitalism (Dobb, 1973).

In his later work, Marx attempted to relate value to price under competitive conditions where profit varies with the amount of capital (machinery) employed, but he did not live to complete *Capital* and his followers have been arguing the application of his theory to advanced industrial capitalism ever since (Meek, 1967; Robinson, 1981; Steedman *et al.*, 1981). A telling example of the invisibility of women in a theory explicitly committed to liberating both sexes is contained in the way this century-long discussion has never paused to give thought to the relationship of essential, non-market reproductive work to market value. It remained for the women's movement to raise the question.

Labor power, in Marxist terms, is a commodity that is consumed in commodity production but it cannot be entirely produced there. In his chapter on simple reproduction, Marx tells us that the worker's individual consumption is 'productive consumption' and 'a factor of the production and reproduction of capital' even if the worker consumes for his own pleasure 'and not to please the capitalist.' He argues that the capitalist profits not only by what he takes from the laborer but what he gives him. Wages are converted into necessities, 'by the consumption of which the muscles, nerves, bones and brains of existing laborers are reproduced, and new labourers are begotten' (p. 626).

Marx was naturally aware that something besides pure consumption went on in the home, even if he expressed it in the passive voice (are converted, are reproduced, are begotten). Nevertheless, the work that converts wages into this continuous cycle of 'productive consumption' is nowhere accounted for in the calculation of surplus value. Marx adds:

> The maintenance and reproduction of the working-class is, and must ever be, a necessary condition to the reproduction of capital. But the capitalist may safely leave its fulfillment to the labourer's instincts of self-preservation and of propagation. (p. 627)

Labor in the home was a given. Together with child-bearing, it had always existed. Just as the free gifts of nature were not included in his model, although Marx had made clear on numerous occasions that he considered them the basis of material wealth, so domestic production and repro-duction fell outside the framework of his analysis of capital-ism. They were part of the ahistorical, external conditions for any mode of production.

Because Marxism is not just an economic theory but a theory of social relationships, the exclusion of this necessary but unrecorded work that happens to be performed by women has had far-reaching consequences for the socialist move-ment and also for the position of women in the Soviet Union and other countries that followed its example. It is not only under capitalism that domestic labor is marginalized.

Marx (1975) made the relationship between men and women the touchstone of the extent to which our animal nature has become human. He found the scientific explan-ation for all alienation to lie not in personal relationships as such, however, but in the relations of material production that put their stamp on all other relations. 'The whole of human servitude,' he wrote in his early *Economic and Philosophical Manuscripts*, written in 1844, 'is involved in the relation of the worker to production, and all relations of servitude are nothing but modifications and consequences of this relation.' Therefore, he said, 'universal human emancipation' is contained in the emancipation of the workers (p. 333).

The understanding of personal relations as totally encompassed by production relations has meant, throughout the history of the socialist movement, that the relationship between men and women could be humanized only through changes in the sphere of commodity production. This is the essence of Engels's (1972) approach in his *The Origin of the Family*, which put forward the Marxist program for the emancipation of women: the 'woman question' will be solved in the public arena of production relations.

Once private property has been abolished, he said, women will be emancipated by being incorporated into the labor force, while private domestic work will be converted into a public industry. The whole area in which the exploitation of women's domestic labor and sexuality takes place simply drops out of sight in this analysis. The dynamics of male–female relationships become a private matter only, and need not concern a revolutionary party.

According to this way of looking at it, once private property has been abolished, there is no longer any conflict of interests between the sexes, and men can speak for women just as well as women can speak for themselves (and just as men always had in revolutionary parties). It is assumed that socialist male aims are synonymous with the aims of all society, and that the working class will reorganize society to take over the housework and child care so that women can enter production. Lenin thought it quite realistic, in 1919, to call for a 'mass struggle' against housework 'led by the proletariat' (1952, p. 233).

As the experience of the Soviet Union and other Eastern European countries amply illustrates, however, after private property is overthrown male priorities continue to be anchored in the categories that are visible to men. It is the 'productive' sphere that creates new values: this means rapid industrial development, big projects, maximum use of resources and absolute faith in technology. It is supposed that funds will trickle down from this kind of growth to take care of housing, public transport and the whole infrastructure of services. But because the whole 'unproductive' business of reproducing the labor force continues to be carried out no matter what, out of sight of the planners and free of charge, investment in its transformation is the Cinderella of every socialist budget. Not only is women's double burden perpetuated; the industrial policies followed have an important limiting effect on the work available to women and on their freedom of choice (H. Scott, 1982c).

The view of housework as petty and unproductive prevailed among socialists, women as well as men, until it began to be challenged in the early 1970s. Margaret Benston (1980) argued in 1969 that housewives were not merely passive consumers but that they played an economic role by producing 'use values' that were consumed at home. They were thus engaged in a precapitalist mode of production. Mariarosa Dalla Costa and Selma James (1975) carried the argument further by declaring that domestic labor actually produced a commodity, labor power, and thus contributed to the production of surplus value.

The 'domestic labor debate' that took place in the mid-1970s, conducted primarily by British Marxists (see, for example, Malos, 1980; Seccombe, 1974; Smith, 1978), could not get beyond this seeming paradox: domestic labor is essential for the reproduction of the capitalist system because it helps to reproduce the labor force, but it does not itself produce surplus value, or profits. This may sound like a contradiction, but it is the only possible conclusion as long as the framework of Marx's argument is preserved.

What gives labor power its value (literally, its 'exchange value') in Marx's analysis, is the quality it has in common with other commodities – not its particular usefulness but its quality of being a product of human labor in the abstract. Domestic labor cannot be expressed as abstract labor, however, because this homogenization of different kinds of labor takes place only on the market, where things have to be equated with each other. Further, the value of a commodity is measured by the 'socially necessary' labor time needed to produce it, but there is no mechanism for establishing the average level of productivity of household work; hence its value cannot be calculated.

In a word, it is not possible to add domestic labor time to waged labor time because one is concrete, individual labor and the other is abstract, homogenized, social labor; they are not the same sort of thing. And if we could add the two it would topple Marx's model; labor power would sell for *less* than its value instead of *at* its value if this unpaid component from outside commodity production were added to it.

The domestic labor debate exasperated more people than it enlightened. The verdict was logical within the terms set, but that logic was difficult to grasp and seemed irrelevant for women to whom it was already obvious that their free work was materially benefiting both husbands and capitalists. The debate pointed up the inability of Marxist theory, and with it left-wing political parties, to accommodate that reality, and it strengthened the conviction among socialist women that Marxism was gender-blind. In spite of Marx's expressed concern for women's oppression, he saw the world through the eyes of the male working class, and this is the view he substituted for the narrow perspective of the entrepreneurial class, who saw labor as a cost of production rather than a value input (to use modern jargon). Marx enlarged the angle of vision, but not enough to illuminate the economics of personal life.

Economics as presently practised exercises its tyranny by forcing us to fit our lives to limited, formal models of reality. It appears to deal with our bread and butter so that we feel that we must listen. Or, in the words of Hazel Henderson (1981), quoted at the beginning of the chapter, it gets in the way of people talking to each other about what is valuable under drastically changed conditions. The consequences for women have proved serious enough, since they are leading to the feminization of poverty.

What can we make out of what we have learned? If working women have a special relationship to production because of the vast store of invisible work that stands between them and the labor market, the answer is certainly not to solve the problem of women's preferential impoverishment by distributing poverty equally between women and men. Is there a way of using the question of unpaid work, of the division of labor, as an instrument for attacking not just the poverty of women but poverty in general? Our approach to unpaid work in the past has been that it was on the way out. We have tried to get it recognized as honorary paid work by having it included in the GNP or smuggling it into Marxist theory, and thus achieving for it some kind of ascriptive value. Many of us have assumed that it would eventually be taken over by the market or by the state and so become official work. This solution now emerges as a dead end.

Having seen where economists' definitions of work and value lead, we no longer want to subject everything we do to the judgement of the market. Schumacher (1973) has summed up the irrationality of submitting all our values to its narrow criteria:

> To press non-economic values into the framework of the economic calculus, economists use the method of cost/benefit analysis. This is generally thought to be an enlightened and progressive development, as it is at least an attempt to take account of costs and benefits which might otherwise be disregarded altogether. In fact, however, it is a procedure by which the higher is reduced to the level of the lower and the priceless is given a price. It can therefore never serve to clarify the situation and lead to an enlightened decision. All it can do is lead to self-deception or to the deception of others; for to undertake to measure the immeasurable is absurd. . . . The logical absurdity, however, is not the greatest fault of the undertaking: what is worse, and destructive of civilization, is the pretence that everything has a price or, in other words, that money is the highest of all values. (pp. 45–6)

Schumacher here is talking about the 'non-economic' values of nature. What he says is just as true for the 'feminine' non-economic values of caring and nurturing. Human services cannot be reduced entirely to economic operations. Ask any mother, writes Jean Bethke Elshtain, whether she would accept 'producing the future commodity labor power' as an apt characterization of what she is doing. One's fears and love for children are drained of meaning . . . when they are recast exclusively as relations between 'reproducers' and 'future labor power.' (1982, p. 614)

Beyond this, there are compelling 'economic' reasons for limiting the sphere governed by conventional economics. As we have seen, there is no way of solving the world's poverty that includes reproducing the West's model of development and type of consumption in the Third World. The minority of the world's people living in industrialized countries has already used up a large piece of the future. Our countries, including those in the Soviet area of influence, will have to change their style-of-life goals in so far as these are dependent on intensive exploitation of natural resources and produce massive pollution problems.

The whole idea that the entire world will eventually live on fast foods transported hundreds of miles in refrigerator trucks burning millions of tons of fuel is nineteenth-century science fiction. We cannot seriously believe that *everyone* is some day going to drive to work in an automobile and that the Sahara desert will be converted into a parking place or a shopping mall. We cannot expect (and probably do not want) all gardening, subsistence farming, cooking, cleaning and home repairs to be taken over by capital-intensive technology the way we have handed the care of our bodies over to capital-intensive medicine.

Of course, all human caring services need to be expanded at the expense of wasteful production, armaments in the first place. Of course we need more and better day care and more possibilities of specialized care for the chronically ill, the disabled and the frail elderly. But the notion that we can socialize all the care of the non-working population in institutions so that all women of working age can travel to typically low-paid female caretaking occupations doesn't make sense for the industrialized West. Try to imagine it as a replacement for the African or Indian village. This has sometimes been described as the taking-in-each-other's-washing model.

The alternative is not going back to the soil and rejecting technology entirely. Neither is it total rejection of the monetized exchange economy that now links the whole world. Certainly it is not going back to telling women that what they do at home is so noble and important that they should stop competing for a place in the public sphere.

What we can insist on, however, is that the 'male' definitions of work and value are no longer the dominant ones, and that 'the human values that women were assigned to preserve expand out of the confines of private life and become the organizing principles of society . . . a society that is organized around human needs' (Ehrenreich and English, 1978, p. 369).

In economic terms, this means that we reject the dichotomy between 'productive' and 'non-productive' work. Instead, we not only aim for the recognition of unpaid work as real work on its own terms, productive of value, but we clear a space for it. To quote Henderson (1981) again: 'The task is that of rebalancing societies so that informal-sector values and functions are revived and restored, while the institutionalized economy and its money values are limited and put back in their place' (p. 369).

Are we talking about some kind of a sentimental utopia? As a matter of fact, many people in the women's movement and out of it are already thinking along these lines, and when all the trends that are taking shape are pulled together it is quite realistic to think in terms of this kind of a social solution.

Chapter 9

TOWARD A POLITICAL ECONOMY OF UNPAID WORK

The time is ripe to think and talk concretely about how to make unpaid work and the values it represents at least as central to our planning as paid work, and in doing so to change the evaluation of paid work as well. This is not an idealist's dream, a panacea for all the world's ills, but a practical necessity.

The concentration on values associated with women's unpaid work (and, records the International Labor Organization, women do 90 per cent of the world's unpaid work) is not in conflict with any peaceful program to transform political and economic structures in the direction of a better distribution of wealth and power, a basic condition for the elimination of poverty. It is an approach to change on which people of diverse political opinions can agree. The political economy of unpaid labor does not draw attention away from the roles played by race and class in 'selecting' the poor; it draws attention, as this book has documented, to causes of poverty that are overlooked in other analyses. It is a different way of looking at solutions that can help us distinguish those that have a potential for real change in the still uncharted world of atomic physics, biotechnology and the microchip, and those that reached the height of their effectiveness in the reign of heavy industry.

'Feminist' thinking, not all of it done by women, has passed through the stage of generalizations about the need to change the prevailing value system based on hard-fisted competition, and has progressed to concrete ideas about how life could be organized in a more human way, and to the identification of potential allies.

Back in 1971, Germaine Greer wrote that

unless the concepts of work and play and reward for work change absolutely, women must continue to provide cheap labour, and even more, free labour exacted of right by an employer possessed of a contract for life, made out in his favour. (p. 22)

In a pamphlet published about the same time, Angela Weir and Elizabeth Wilson (1973) rejected the notion that politics for the women's movement could be limited to alternative lifestyles as a form of protest, or to conventional workplace demands, or to piecemeal struggles on individual issues like the right to abortion and free contraceptives.

They wrote that they wanted to see the distinction between work and leisure transcended:

What we rebel against is the separation of work from enjoyment, and of home from work. Nor do we want individual men taking over some of 'our' jobs in the home while we take over some of 'his' in the office or factory. We want greater flexibility between work and home – to have our kids with us at our place of work, or to work at home; we want greater flexibility in our concepts of what is mental and what is manual labour, and also of the nature of skills. (pp. 92–3).

These thoughts occur again and again in women's writings of the 1970s. The old idea of equality – the right to be judged by monetary values and criteria of success just like men, to join the dehumanizers instead of being dehumanized – gave way to an insistence on new social visions. Herbert Marcuse (1972) was one of the male thinkers who saw the radical power in the feminist movement provided it did not settle for sharing the spoils of male-dominated society but set its sights on the negation of 'male' principles and the 'feminization' of the male. Roger Garaudy, for decades a leading ideologist of the French Communist Party, was another who declared 'the feminist critique of industrialism, socialist and capitalist, the only fundamentally innovative analysis available' (Henderson, 1981, p. 375).

Swedish women were among the very first to recognize the importance of making the 'humanization of men' the center of political struggle. As early as the mid-1950s, women theoreticians were talking about the need for men to reenter human space and of the possibility of breaking down stereotyped sex roles so that men and women could share equally in the public and private spheres. The difficulty of achieving this transformation, even in a welfare state dedicated to social policies designed to equalize roles, as long as the prevailing philosophy of the major political parties is the conventional one of production, power and profits, is the lesson of Sweden's 'sex-role equality program' launched in 1968 (H. Scott, 1982a).

A more human society will not be built on a trade-off: more jobs for women, more baby care for men. As the Swedish sociologist Rita Liljeström observed after a decade of experience with this 'sex-role equality' model:

> Women, if they are to achieve their collective liberation, need to rally around a community of values, around a program which roots them in shared experiences and which gives them political identity for 'sisterhood' and an alternative value system to keep them from being devoured by an equality under the terms set by the male value system. For women's liberation is about something more than 'to pass off as a man.' It is about changing destructive features in a man's society. (H. Scott, 1982a, p. 157)

Angela Miles (1981), in an analysis of what she sees as the new feminist political perspective, locates the beginnings of conscious expression of what she calls the 'integrative feminist principle' in the mid-1970s, eventually uniting all feminist tendencies except the radical separatist and the orthodox Marxist. While this principle, like the Swedish goal of sex-role equality, assumes an alternative definition of human nature that includes and values both 'male' and 'female' characteristics, it goes further than the Swedish model. It holds that the transcendence of the division between the personal and the political, paid and unpaid work, monetized and non-monetized values, work and leisure, production and reproduction, can be the basis of a 'general synthesizing perspective of universal significance' (p. 486). For Miles, the development of this alternative value framework marks the shift of feminism from a politics of pressure representing the interests of a specific group to a complete alternative politics with reference to the whole of society and with universal relevance for the shape and direction of progressive struggle in general in this period. (p. 481)

Another sociologist, Margaret L. Andersen, sees a similar coming together of liberal, socialist and radical feminist perspectives, regardless of their differences, behind the goals of a society without

race, gender, and class distinctions in the production and distribution of property or economic resources . . . where power is not distributed by virtue of one's class, race, or gender and where individual civil rights are respected and maintained. And finally, such a society would have to respect and encourage traditional female values, but not restrict them to only one-half of the population, who, by virtue of their gender, are categorized as subordinate to the other. . . . (p. 295)

This is not yet a 'complete alternative politics' and it is more of a manifesto than a program. Yet the outlines for a 'female' society surface with increasing frequency and the proposals have many general features in common: the involvement of both sexes in the care of others, thought of as including work at home or in the community; a broader definition of work; more flexible use of time; smaller-scale, more human working and living arrangements.

Studies made both in the US and Sweden indicate that women prefer to work near their home, they favor part-time jobs and job sharing. Women do not want to travel long distances, work overtime, or be slaves to their jobs because they rarely lose sight of the needs of children. They like working in non-hierarchical, decentralized, small work-places where work can be organized without power games (Edsta, 1981; Klemesrud, 1981; H. Scott, 1982a). They prefer their jobs to involve relationships with people even when they are successful career women. Carol Gilligan (1982), a professor of psychology at Harvard, reports this as a typical reaction of capable professional women. She describes the doctor who fears success because she believes it will make it impossible to spend time with her patients; she likes to visit them after hours. Women lawyers are unhappy with the adversary system of fighting cases because of their concern for losers as well as winners. Gilligan views this humanization of work attitudes as positive.

Evidence continues to accumulate that not all men are interested in making it in the rat race. Andrée Michel, Research Director of the National Center of Scientific Research in Paris, reports that an increasing number of French men are seeking jobs through agencies that place temporary workers. They do not want to make a lifetime commitment to elbowing their way up the ladder. According to Swedish figures, one-quarter of fathers now take some time off from work to stay home with a new baby during its first year. The demand for increasing participation of fathers in child care has spread so rapidly that in 1981 the International Labour Organization adopted Recommendation. 165 urging governments to make it possible for either parent to obtain parental leave without loss of job rights (Janjic, 1983).

A book entitled *Life and Death on the Corporate Battlefield* by Solman and Friedman (1982) that has no higher moral purpose than to satisfy the curiosity of would-be entrepreneurs about how the successful get ahead, devotes twenty pages to the way the Harvard School of Business teaches students to look out for Number One by playing competitive games. If the 'killer instinct' is that hard to inculcate, one can assume that many men survive without it. One such man is James Robertson (1981), a former British government expert with, as he describes it, policy-making powers. After disillusionment with public service and years spent in a 'near frenzy of reformist activity,' he writes,

I began to question the assumption that social progress can be made by reforming the institutions and institutional processes and relationships of society, as if these formed a system external to and independent of ourselves as persons. I began to see this as a specifically 'masculine' assumption, and to feel that it was deeply false. (p. 84)

He contrasts the HE (hyper-expansionist) view of post-industrial society with the SHE (sane, humane, ecological) future. The first he describes as 'Utopian projection fantasies of the male technocratic elites': they rely on space coloniz-ation, nuclear power, automation, genetic engineering and behavioral manipulation to overcome all social and economic problems and ensure unlimited material growth (pp. 85–6).

The second, SHE view of post-industrial society emphasizes human rather than economic growth. It will promote self-reliance, self-sufficiency and appropriate tech-nologies that will conserve resources and the environment. The trend will be toward more small decentralized manu-facture, more small farming and individual food growing, more community responsibility for health and education and 'more living and working together by children, young people, adults, and the elderly' (p. 87). In other words, we will live more of our lives in the informal economy. This will not be done by rejecting the advantages of technology but by using it to change direction:

There will be further automation of drudgework in large manufacturing and service enterprises; more people will work on food growing and in small businesses; there will be a shift toward part-time paid work; working people will have more free time; there will be more equal distribution of paid and unpaid work between men and women; higher status will be attached to socially useful work, including unpaid work that is socially useful; and measures will be introduced to provide unpaid workers with a money income otherwise than from their work. (p. 87)

A similar non-patriarchal model is put forward by Prof. Josef Huber of the Free University in Berlin, who sees both men and women working part-time in the future, sharing child care and other social duties, with people performing community services voluntarily that are at present carried out by government bureaucracies (Henderson, 1981). If these projections seem to refer back to the Utopian societies inspired in the nineteenth century by Robert Owen, Claude Henri de Saint-Simon and Charles Fourier, it is certainly true that they draw on this tradition but with important differences. They do not rely on unpaid women to supply all the maintenance, childrearing and personal services; and they suggest an alternative at a time when the chances for most people of living in the monetized economy alone are diminishing, and when the conventional pattern of industrialization is choking life rather than sustaining it or opening up new vistas of the good life as it did in the nineteenth and early twentieth centuries.

One government has started to take this approach seriously. If Sweden wants to maintain the present level of public care services to children, the ill and disabled, the elderly and the disadvantaged into the next century, it will have to make use of the unpaid work of private citizens to supplement that of professionals. This is the conclusion of a five-year study called 'Care in Sweden' by the Swedish governmental Secretariat for Future Studies published in 1982 (Lagergren, 1983). The report proposes a changed work pattern – shared job opportunities, shorter paid working time alternating with other, unpaid occupations – as a solution that would also deal with the certainty that the 'labor surplus' will continue to grow. Several hundred thousand private sector jobs will disappear in this small country by the end of the century.

For Sweden to maintain the present level of welfare entirely by adding paid personnel would mean doubling costs over the 1982 level by the year 2000, a prohibitive increase in view of the slow rate of industrial growth projected, the borrowing against the future that has already taken place, and the extent of present commitments that were planned for a high-growth society. But this is not the only disadvantage of 'further professionalization' of care.

The study found serious shortcomings in the way professional services meet their clients' needs. Impersonal, superficial, short-term, and at the same time overprotective; failure to make use of people's own resources – these were the criticisms levelled at the way the model welfare state delivers its services. Another finding was that everyday care given by individuals to members of their family, to friends and neighbors, totalled more than care in the public sector, but that this time was distributed very unevenly. Parents of small children were overburdened, while other people were completely uninvolved.

Mårten Lagergren (1983), the project director, concludes:

> If we reduce working hours, nobody will need to accept a meaningless job for the sake of employment. If we share the work of care, everybody will be able to obtain all the care they need. We will not need to keep the machinery of care going for the sake of employment, nor will we have to sacrifice an unreasonable proportion of our income paying others to do the work of care for us. (p. 9)

It is the failure of the growth model, so long admired by capital and labor, rather than concern that women are getting a raw deal, that has encouraged this new interest in 'use values.' The elevation of 'women's values' to world values means simply a strengthening of the use values of caring, humanizing activities which are done largely by women. This is why the new politicalization of feminist theory and the trend toward organizing coherently to realize 'female' aims is now seen by some forward-looking men as well as by women as having broad application. There is a growing sense that what is 'radical,' in the sense of getting at the root of things, has changed.

The political potential of an unexpected set of issues emerged, for example, with the recognition in the US of a 'gender gap' in the 1982 congressional elections: the discovery of an independent women's vote with a 'disapproval margin' of as much as twenty points between women's and men's opinions on President Reagan's policies as measured by opinion polls. There is, of course, a danger in becoming beguiled by a single political phenomenon. Nevertheless, it is one that indicates a shift in the location of effective pressure points.

Take, for example, the long struggle in the US around the Equal Rights Amendment to the Constitution. The ERA, dismissed by much of the political left as a middle-class issue pressed by middle-class women, actually focused attention as no other campaign had ever previously done on women's issues among people who had until then never thought there was such a thing. Although the ERA simply restates a principle that is already expressed in federal laws, that there shall be no discrimination for reasons of sex, and is not likely to improve women's position, the fight for its passage has clarified some of the reasons for women's low status for many ordinary people and for at least some of their political representatives throughout the US.

Eventually it became impossible to talk about 'discrimination for reasons of sex' without talking about women's jobs, women's pay, women's poverty, the extreme disadvantages of minority women, the hungry, the homeless and poverty in general. Women's opposition to defense spending, the need to restore welfare cuts and social services, inclusion of jobs for women in employment-creation programs, discrimination against women in civil service and social security legislation, tax breaks for single parents – these became issues on which some congressmen and state officials were at least prepared to listen as women were perceived to have voting clout that cut across party lines.

Men learned that they can no longer count on women absorbing male stances as soon as they come within reach of male power. The results of a study by the Center for the American Woman and Politics at Rutgers University revealed that women public officials, regardless of party, take more liberal positions than their male counterparts. Black women, moreover, are more liberal than all other elected women officials. These lessons were not lost on the six major candidates for the Democratic presidential nomination who appeared at the 1983 conference of the National Organization for Women with ringing endorsements of women's issues.

The politicians may or may not deliver on their promises, and politics need not be left to the politicians. The women's movement has potential allies in the campaign to elevate women's values: the black and other minority movements, the peace movement and the environmental movement, in all of which women already play a prominent part and which are directly involved in the paramount issues of our time: survival, in the short and long term, and the fight against poverty.

You don't need to be a mathematician to understand that every reduction in military spending could mean an increase in spending on human welfare, and that every increase in military spending increases the danger of extinction as well as exacerbating world poverty. Marian Wright Edelman, a black lawyer and president of the Children's Defense Fund in Washington, DC, told girls graduating from Milton Academy in 1983 that worldwide 40,000 children die every year from malnutrition, and that poverty is the ultimate cause of death of 11,000 American children annually. In that year, she pointed out, the US was spending 24 million dollars an hour on defense (*The New Yorker*, 27 June 1983). The world as a whole felt able to afford 600 billion dollars for military expenditures in 1982 (Sivard, 1982), up 200 billion since 1976. Yet a mere 12.5 billion dollars annually, in 1974 prices, between 1975 and 1985 would have ensured minimum human needs in the Third World in terms of nutrition, education, housing, drinking water, health and family planning and transport (Haq, 1976). Even allowing for inflation, the entire sum for 1984 could have been met from the increase in US arms spending alone.

Three-quarters of the world's trade in armaments is with the Third World, the US and the USSR being the main suppliers. Between 1960 and 1982 sixty-five major wars were fought, most of them in the Third World. Virtually half the national governments in developing countries are dominated by the military, Sivard (1982) points out, and the proliferation of weapons is such that it is virtually impossible to imagine the peaceful and permanent transfer of power to a more representative form of government.

Peace, protection of the environment and a lifestyle stressing human values are inextricably linked. Assuming that we are all still here in the 1990s, the major challenge will be how to ensure an energy supply for the future and at the same time preserve the environment and the world's resources. Even if the movement to limit the use of nuclear power should be successful and the problem of the disposal of nuclear wastes could be dealt with, there would still be side effects from the combustion of oil and coal, the worst of which is the acidification of land and water. Even renewable sources of energy have environmental effects (wind, biomass, water, etc.). Our resources are further threatened by chemical processes and products, car emissions, noise and the over-exploitation of agricultural land and forests.

Who will ensure that today's struggles against the negative effects of growth and of arms spending, in so far as they are successful, will be transformed into positive programs incorporating the redefinition and reevaluation of work? Both the peace movement and the environmental movement have depended on the physical support of women – on their willingness to put their bodies on the line. Greenham Common will be remembered as the place where women did just that, and not for days but for years, in an effort to stop the deployment of missiles on that site in Britain. Yet few women have made themselves experts on the technological and political issues involved in disarmament or transforming a war-based economy to a peace economy.

An attempt to locate women disarmament specialists by Elise Boulding (1981), a sociologist with a special interest in peace research, turned up sixty-three professionally engaged women in nineteen countries; not an impressive figure even allowing for the fact that Boulding was not able to undertake an exhaustive search.

Neither are enough women training to serve in the ranks of decision makers at all levels about how technology is to be used in the future, whether on problems directly involving the environment or those related to planning and executing production programs in general. Many women seem content to believe that women's values will receive recognition primarily through involving more men in work with people, particularly in parenting. It is assumed that this would produce men less inclined to use technology for aggressive aims and women more oriented toward technical problem-solving, and so it might. It is a long shot, however, and a very long-term solution, and in the meanwhile the possibilities for involving more women in technology through a different kind of education have been by no means exhausted.

Evelyn Fox Keller (1982), a mathematician and philosopher of science, sympathizes with the many women who find themselves strangers in the realm of establishment science and technology, but she deplores the particular strand of feminist thinking that leads from questioning its claim to absolute knowledge to the rejection of science as such and of the possibility of understanding the world in rational terms. This is, she says,

> the kind of radical move that transforms the political spectrum into a circle. By rejecting objectivity as a masculine ideal, it simultaneously lends its voice to an enemy chorus and dooms women to residing outside the realpolitik modern culture; it exacerbates the very problem it wishes to solve. (p. 593)

There can be no plan for the utilization of human 'use values' that does not recognize that technology is necessary to make this possible. Not even the most avid organic gardener envisions a world without power-driven equipment, labor-saving devices, mass-produced articles, transportation, refrigeration, communications and so on. The issue is not whether there will be technology but how it will be used. The political scientist Victor Ferkiss (1974) is convincingly emphatic about this:

> Women and men of the future will not be able to escape from the all-pervading influence of technology – whether of the work-performing or communicating variety – for the simple reason that by the twenty-first century the world will be incapable of supporting the vast population which is already inevitable (barring worldwide catastrophe) without the use of highly advanced technology. The coming 7 to 8 billion human beings – almost half of whom are already here – cannot all be fed by organically grown foods marketed locally by small farmers, cannot be clothed by homespun animal or vegetable fibres, and cannot be sheltered in local wood or stone. . . . The alternative to technological growth and development is even more widespread poverty than now exists. . . . The problem of the twenty-first century will not be whether to accept or reject technological civilization as such but how to order it to truly human ends. (p. 17)

The perspective is not to recruit women for science and

technology as they are practised today, but by involving women to change the way these fields are organized, the questions they ask, the problems they decide to solve, and the way they go about solving them. A woman biologist, Anne Fausto-Sterling (1981), writes:

> To imagine a future with women integrated into science is to imagine a culture transformed. Such a society would value different kinds of work equally. It would insist that science, the key to understanding the natural world in which we live, be accessible to everyone. Scientific research would no longer be practiced by individual entrepreneurs. Rather, ways of allowing the majority of citizens to set priorities and goals for research projects would have to exist. (p. 49)

The trade unions, in spite of their past record on women's issues, are an important potential ally in the coming movement to elevate the worth of unpaid labor and distribute it more evenly. In the US the unions have been slower than in some other countries to recognize that in the present period of permanent industrial crisis the traditional working-class demands for higher pay and better fringe benefits, fought with the traditional strike weapon, are not addressing the crucial issue – permanent unemployment. Unions have found themselves in the embarrassing position of supporting defense spending because it creates jobs, and of closing their eyes to pollution because more jobs were at stake. Labor organizations that think only in terms of short-term guarantees for their own membership are losing bargaining power along with members in the face of mass lay-offs produced by automation. This is particularly true in the US where only about one-quarter of the labor force is unionized, and many unemployed women and men do not feel that their interests coincide with those of organized labor.

In Europe some unions as well as governments and Common Market officials have been talking for at least ten years in terms of an inevitable shift toward a shorter work week and job sharing. The governments of Belgium, France, Italy and the Netherlands have already legislated reduced hours and flexible work-sharing schemes, or are in the process of negotiating them. The European Trade Union Confederation has called for a European 35-hour week, and the EEC Commission has recommended the reorganization of work schedules and a reduction in working time.

West German experts have estimated that simply by extending schooling for a year, lowering retirement age by a year, shortening the work week by one hour, adding one day of holiday per year, and giving every tenth worker a two-week educational leave, one million jobs could be created. The powerful metal workers' union is pressing for a 35-hour week without a reduction in pay. In Britain it has been calculated that a 35-hour week could add 500,000 jobs. The UK National Union of Mineworkers is proposing a four-day week, early retirement, and an end to overtime, as a way to halt firings and create new jobs in the nationalized coal industry.

Employers have in the main opposed these changes, but some companies see shorter work schedules as inevitable and have introduced them at least experimentally. Pressure for different ways of organizing work will be created by new technology as well as by unemployment. Yet it is unlikely that the goal of full or almost full employment will be realized simply by reductions in working hours not related to other changes. Giles Merritt (1982), a London *Financial Times* writer, cites a European survey of employers indicating that almost two-thirds would use shorter hours to reduce the workforce permanently through further rationalization and the use of overtime – in other words, would 'take the money and run' (p. 157). He writes:

> Beyond any reasonable doubt, during the years of the 1980s there is no foreseeable power on earth that can generate enough real peacetime jobs to satisfy demand enough to keep OECD joblessness down at around 25 million people. *Therefore jobs must be created that are not real work.* (p. 173) (my italics – H.S.)

Although Merritt considers any work not generated in the private sector as 'not real work,' he nevertheless strongly advocates the creation of jobs by government-funded construction projects to alleviate the housing crisis in the US and

Europe. He stresses that jobs should be created in areas that produce marketable products, and not in services which, in his opinion, are money down the drain since they do not stimulate demand and spending in the private sector.

This is the kind of reasonable-sounding job creation proposal that governments are likely to come up with in coming years since they will have to deal with the problem of mass unemployment and poverty in some way. The trouble with it is that it would at best take us back to where we were in the mid-1970s. It does not deal with the long-term consequences of technological development – the inevitable disappearance of jobs in the monetized sector and the vast possibilities for expanding human services and useful activities in the informal sector. It would leave women still doing most of the unpaid work, waiting around for low-paid secondary jobs, still the economically most vulnerable half of the population.

A positive alternative could be put forward by a coalition of women, minorities, peace and environmental movements and labor if they could agree on some common goals and immediate aims. Government spending would be diverted from defense to develop ecologically safe sources of energy and to improve the infrastructure and finance needed public caring services. A universal shorter paid work week would result in more jobs for more people; at the same time these jobs would be evaluated according to the principle of equal pay for *comparable work*. This principle, far from being unworkable as many suppose, is actually being enforced in the case of some state government workers in the US. It is a landmark in the fight against wage discrimination, and it also represents a shift in the cultural climate. The evaluation of jobs according to skill level and accountability helps to break the link between gender and value and may have an unexpectedly great influence on our thinking about how to assess work.

With a shorter work day, people would have time for training or retraining for both paid and unpaid skills. Men as well as women would be involved in voluntary unpaid work, not simply 'sharing parenting' or 'sharing the housework,' but helping to expand all services on a community basis.

Much voluntary work with children, the elderly and the retarded, is already being done, especially by women, in addition to unpaid work in the home. There is no reason to suppose that men would not engage in more of this work if it were to become socially acceptable to do so. Indeed, unpaid rather than paid work might become the key to status:

If long-range predictions about the declining centrality of work and the increasing importance of nonwork activities in cybernated societies became reality, the relevance of paid occupation for class placement may decline, and other, unpaid activities may become more important as a source of social identity. (Acker, 1973, p. 179)

Income would no longer be tied entirely to paid work. Needs would be judged individually, not according to family status. At least some services would no longer be income-related. Recompense for voluntary work could include health insurance, old age and disability pensions, and credit for relevant experience when applying for a job in the monetized sector. Those who gave their time free might also be entitled to free or low-cost access to other facilities, including restaurants, public transportation, recreation and entertainment.

Such changes, begun in the industrial world, would be consistent with a changed policy toward the Third World, the beginning of a situation in which developing countries could decide their own future, with aid tailored to their needs and not ours.

There are already some signs that organized labor is willing to go beyond its traditional demands for a bigger share of the cake. For example:

the support of UK and West German trade unions for nuclear disarmament and the peace movement;

the change of attitude by Swedish unions and their political arm, the Social Democratic Party, toward nuclear power and the 1980 decision, following a national referendum, to phase out nuclear power by the year 2010;

in the US the support of the AFL–CIO for the 1983 'Jobs, Peace, Freedom' march in Washington, DC, in contrast to their refusal to endorse its predecessor in 1963, an occasion made memorable by Martin Luther King's 'I Have a Dream' speech;

the success of the campaign for recognition of equal pay for comparable work in the state of Washington. The victory of the American Federation of State, Country and Municipal Workers, which represents one million members of whom 400,000 are women, requires the state government to institute the same wage scales for comparable jobs (e.g., for secretaries and maintenance carpenters; licensed practical nurses and correctional officers). The decision will raise pay checks for female state employees by an average of 31 per cent.

A long look at the feminization of poverty has suggested an approach that could help alleviate poverty in general. At the same time it meets the urgent need for a completely different way of thinking about how life in industrial society could be organized. The 'female' values it stresses are those associated with life, in contrast to the values associated with death and poverty that are increasingly dominating our lives. The elevation of unpaid work to a place in the economy equal to that of paid work can make of improved human welfare in the general sense an economically practical goal. Thus it goes beyond obvious short-term proposals for work projects, unemployment benefits, restoration of welfare cuts and strengthening of individual social policies, desirable as these aims are.

It would be naïve to imagine that any such transformation in our value system can take place in a short time or without political confrontations. In the long term, profound changes in the structure of our society will be necessary. Nevertheless it is possible to work on individual goals without accepting a particular blueprint for change in advance. These include peace, disarmament, environmental protection, socially safe and useful technologies and ways of making scientific and technological knowledge and skills more accessible; narrower goals like the shorter work week, parental leave and equal pay for comparable work; and projects involving alternative forms of care or exchange of services. There are possibilities for everyone who wants not just material security but better human relationships to contribute at their own pace and in the field of their choice.

The political economy of unpaid work is open to almost infinite elaboration by people with the imagination to start discussing it today.

BIBLIOGRAPHY

Acker, J. (1973), 'Women and social stratification: a case of intellectual sexism', in J. Huber (ed.), *Changing Women in a Changing Society*, Chicago, University of Chicago Press, pp. 174–83.

Adams, H. F. (1983), 'Work in the interstices: women in academe', *Women's Studies International Forum*, vol. 6, no. 2, pp. 134–42.

Aguilar-San Juan, D. (1982), 'Feminism and the national liberation struggle in the Philippines', *Women's Studies International Forum*, vol. 5, nos. 3–4, pp. 253–61.

Aldrich, M. (1978), 'Women in science: review essay', *Signs*, vol. 4, no. 1, pp. 126–35.

Al-Hibri, A. (1981), 'Capitalism is an advanced stage of patriarchy: but marxism is not feminism', in L. Sargent (ed.), *Women and Revolution*, Boston, South End Press, pp. 165–93.

Al-Hibri, A. (1982), 'A study of Islamic herstory: or how did we ever get into this mess?', *Women's Studies International Forum*, vol. 5, no. 2, pp. 207–20.

Alic, M. (1981), 'Women and technology in ancient Alexandria: Maria and Hypatia', *Women's Studies International Quarterly*, vol. 4, no. 3, pp. 305–12.

Almquist, E. (1979), *Minorities, Gender and Work*, Lexington, Mass., Lexington Books.

Andersen, M. L. (1983), *Thinking About Women: Sociological and Feminist Perspectives*, New York, Macmillan.

Anderson, M. B. (1983), 'Technology transfer and development: implications for women', manuscript, publication forthcoming.

Arizpe, L. (1977), 'Women in the informal labor sector: the case of Mexico City, *Signs*, vol. 3, no. 1, pp. 25–37.

Arizpe, L. and Aranda, J. (1981), 'The "comparative advantages" of women's disadvantages: women workers in the strawberry export business in Mexico City', *Signs*, vol. 7, no. 2, pp. 453–73.

Armstrong, P. (n.d.), 'Women and unemployment', *Working Papers*, Ottawa, Canadian Research Institute for the Advancement of Women.

Arnold, E., Birke, L. and Faulkner, W. (1981), 'Women and microelectronics: the case of word processors', *Women's Studies International Quarterly*, vol. 4, no. 3, pp. 321–40.

Balogh, T. (1982), *The Irrelevance of Conventional Economics*, New York, Liveright.

Bebel, A. (1971), *Women Under Socialism*, New York, Schocken Books (first published 1879).

Benenson, H. (1984), 'A critique of the dual-career family analysis', *British Journal of Sociology*, vol. 40, no. 1, pp. 19–41.

Benston, M. (1980), 'The political economy of women's labour', in E. Malos (ed.), *The Politics of Housework*, London, Allison & Busby, pp. 119–29.

Bird, E. (1980), *Information Technology in the Office: the Impact on Women's Jobs*, Manchester, Equal Opportunities Commission.

Blau, F. D. and Jusenius, C. L. (1980), 'Economists' approaches to sex segregation in the labor market: an appraisal', in M. Blaxall and B. Reagan (eds), *Women and the Workplace*, Chicago, University of Chicago Press, pp. 181–200.

Blaxall, M. and Reagan, B. (eds) (1980), *Women and the Workplace*, Chicago, University of Chicago Press.

Blumberg, R. L. (1976), 'Kibbutz women: from the fields of revolution to the laundries of discontent', in L. B. Iglitzin and R. R. Ross (eds), *Women in the World*, Santa Barbara, Cal., Clio Press, pp. 319–44.

Bose, C. (1979), 'Technology and changes in the division of labor in the American home', *Women's Studies International Quarterly*, vol. 2, no. 3, pp. 295–304.

Boserup, E. (1970), *Women's Role in Economic Development*, New York, St Martin's Press.

Bothmer, L. von (1978), 'Women and politics', *International Journal of Sociology*, vol. 8, no. 3, pp. 96–111.

Boulding, E. (1976), *The Underside of History*, Boulder, Col., Westview Press.

Boulding, E. (1980), 'Foreword', in N. J. Sokoloff, *Between Money and Love: The Dialectics of Women's Home and Market Work*, New York, Praeger, pp. v–viii.

Boulding, E. (1981), 'Perspectives of women researchers on disarmament, national security, and world order', *Women's Studies International Quarterly*, vol. 4, no. 1, pp. 27–40.

Braverman, H. (1974), *Labor and Monopoly Capital*, New York, Monthly Review Press.

Bridenthal, R. and Koonz, C. (eds) (1977), *Becoming Visible: Women in European History*, Boston and London, Houghton Mifflin.

Bronowski, J. (1973), *The Ascent of Man*, Boston and Toronto, Little Brown.

Brownlee, W. E. (1979), 'Household values, women's work, and economic growth, 1800–1930', *Journal of Economic History*, vol. 39, no. 1, pp. 199–210.

Brownmiller, S. (1976), *Against Our Will*, New York, Bantam Books.

Buvinić, M. (1976), *Women and World Development: An Annotated Bibliography*, Washington, DC, Overseas Development Council.

Caplan, A. P. (1979), 'Indian women: model and reality. A review of recent books, 1975–1979', *Women's Studies International Quarterly*, vol. 2, no. 4, pp. 461–80.

Capra, F. (1982), *The Turning Point*, New York, Simon & Schuster.

Carroll, B. E. (ed.) (1976), *Liberating Women's History*, Urbana, Ill., University of Illinois Press.

Casey, K. (1976), 'The Cheshire cat: reconstructing the experience of medieval women', in B. A. Carroll (ed.), *Liberating Women's History*, Urbana, Ill., University of Illinois Press, pp. 224–49.

Cater, L. A. and Scott, A. F. (eds) (1976), *Women and Men: Changing Roles, Relationships and Perceptions*, New York, Aspen Institute.

Cebotarev, E. A. (1982), 'Research on rural women: an international perspective', *Resources for Feminist Research*, vol. 11, no. 1, pp. 28–32.

Cebotarev, E. A. *et al.* (1982), 'An annotated bibliography on women in agriculture and rural societies', *Resources for Feminist Research*, vol. 11, no. 1, pp. 93–180.

Chacko, A. (1980), 'Traditions die hard', Worldpaper, July/August, p. 5.

Chodorow, N. (1978), *The Reproduction of Mothering*, Berkeley, University of California Press.

Clark, A. (1982), *Working Life of Women in the Seventeenth Century*, London, Boston and Melbourne, Routledge & Kegan Paul (first published 1919).

Comer, L. (1978), 'The question of women and class', *Women's Studies International Quarterly*, vol. 1, no. 2, pp. 165–73.

Cott, N. F. (1978), *The Bonds of Womanhood: 'Women's Sphere' in New England, 1780–1835*, New Haven and London, Yale University Press.

Coulson, M., Magas, B. and Wainwright, H. (1980), ' "The housewife and her labour under capitalism" – a critique', in E. Malos (ed.), *The Politics of Housework*, London, Allison & Busby, pp. 218–34.

Dahlberg, F. (ed.) (1981), *Woman the Gatherer*, New Haven and London, Yale University Press.

Dalla Costa, M. and James, S. (1975), *The Power of Women and the Subversion of the Community*, Bristol, Falling Wall Press.

Daly, M. (1973), *Beyond God the Father*, Boston, Beacon Press.

Dauber, R. and Cain, M. L. (eds) (1981), *Women and Technological Change in Developing Countries*, Boulder, Col., Westview Press.

De Beauvoir, S. (1971), *The Second Sex*, New York, Alfred A. Knopf.

Dinnerstein, D. (1977), *The Mermaid and the Minotaur*, New York, Harper & Row.

Dobb, M. (1973), *Theories of Value and Distribution Since Adam Smith*, Cambridge, New York and Melbourne, Cambridge University Press.

D'Onofrio-Flores, P. M. (1982), 'Technology, economic development, and the division of labour by sex', in P. M. D'Onofrio-Flores and S. M. Pfafflin (eds), *Scientific–Technological Change and the Role of Women in Development*, Boulder, Col., Westview Press, pp. 13–28.

D'Onofrio-Flores, P. M. and Pfafflin, S. M. (eds) (1982), *Scientific–Technological Change and the Role of Women in Development*, Boulder, Col., Westview Press.

Edsta, B. (1981), 'Equal opportunities at work through practical experimentation', *Current Sweden*, no. 265, Stockholm, the Swedish Institute.

Ehrenreich, B. and English, D. (1978), *For Her Own Good: 150 Years of the Experts' Advice to Women*, Garden City, New York, Anchor Books.

Eisenstein, Z. (ed.) (1979), *Capitalism, Patriarchy, and the Case for Socialist Feminism*, New York, Monthly Review Press.

Eisenstein, Z. (1982), 'The sexual politics of the new right: understanding the "crisis of liberalism" for the 1980's', *Signs*, vol. 7, no. 3, pp. 567–88.

Ekejiuba, F. I. (1977), 'Women and symbolic systems: introduction', *Signs*, vol. 3, no. 1, pp. 90–2.

Elmendorf, M. (1976), 'The dilemma of peasant women: a view from a village in Yucatan', in I. Tinker and M. B. Bramsen (eds), *Women and Development*, Washington, DC, Overseas Development Council, pp. 88–94.

El Saadawi, N. (1982), 'Woman and Islam', *Women's Studies International Forum*, vol. 5, no. 2, pp. 193–206.

Elshtain, J. B. (1982), 'Feminist discourse and its discontents: language, power and meaning', *Signs*, vol. 7, no. 3, pp. 603–21.

Elshtain, J. B. (1983), 'Symmetry and soporofics: a critique of feminist theories of gender development', manuscript, publication forthcoming.

Elson, D. and Pearson, R. (1981), 'The subordination of women and the internationalisation of factory production', in K. Young, C. Wolkowitz and R. McCullagh (eds), *Of Marriage and the Market*, London, CSE Books, pp. 144–66. New edition (1984), London, Boston and Melbourne, Routledge & Kegan Paul.

Engels, F. (1953 edn), 'The condition of the working class in England', in *K. Marx and F. Engels On Britain*, Moscow, Foreign Languages Publishing House, pp. 1–336.

Engels, F. (1972 edn), *The Origin of the Family, Private Property and the State*, New York, International Publishers.

Equal Opportunities Commission (1981), *Sixth Annual Report*, Manchester.

Estioko-Griffin, A. and Griffin, P. B. (1981), 'Woman the hunter: the Agta', in F. Dahlberg (ed.), *Woman the Gatherer*, New Haven and London, Yale University Press, pp. 121–51.

Faithorn, E. (1975), 'The concept of pollution among the Káfe of the Papua New Guinea highlands', in R. R. Reiter (ed.), *Toward an Anthropology of Women*, New York, Monthly Review Press, pp. 127–40.

Fausto-Sterling, A. (1981), 'Women and science', *Women's Studies International Quarterly*, vol. 4, no. 1, pp. 41–50.

Feldstiner, M. L. (1980), 'Seeing *The Second Sex* through the Second Wave', *Feminist Studies*, vol. 6, no. 2, pp. 247–76.

Ferkiss, V. C. (1974), *The Future of Technological Civilization*, New York, George Braziller.

Firestone, S. (1971), *The Dialectics of Sex*, New York, Bantam Books.

Flexner, E. (1979), *Century of Struggle: The Women's Rights Movement in the United States*, Cambridge, Mass. and London, Belknap Press.

Foner, P. A. (1947), *History of the Labor Movement in the United States*, New York, International Publishers.

Fröbel, F., Heinrichs, J. and Kreye, O. (1980), *The New International Division of Labor: Structural Unemployment in Industrializing Countries and Industrialization in Developing Countries*, Cambridge, New York and Melbourne, Cambridge University Press.

Gage, M. (1972), *Woman, Church and State*, New York, Arno Press.

Galbraith, J. K. (1958), *The Affluent Society*, Boston and London, Houghton Mifflin.

Galbraith, J. K. (1979), *The Nature of Mass Poverty*, Cambridge, Mass., Harvard University Press.

Gardiner, J., Himmelweit, S. and Mackintosh, M. (1980), 'Women's domestic labour', in E. Malos (ed.), *The Politics of Housework*, London, Allison & Busby, pp. 235–52.

Gilligan, C. (1982), *In a Different Voice*, Cambridge, Mass., Harvard University Press.

Glazer, N. Y. (n.d.), 'The invisible intersection: involuntary unpaid labor outside the household and women workers', Center for the Study, Education and Advancement of Women, University of California, Berkeley, unpublished manuscript.

Glucklich, P. and Snell, M. (1982), *Women, Work and Wages*, Low Pay Unit Discussion Series no. 2, London, Low Pay Unit.

Goldschmidt-Clermont, L. (1982), *Unpaid Work in the Household*, Geneva, International Labor Organization.

Goldschmidt-Clermont, L. (1983), 'Does housework pay? A product-related, microeconomic approach', *Signs*, vol. 9, no. 1, pp. 108–19.

Gordon, D. M. (1972), *Theories of Poverty and Unemployment*, Lexington, Mass., Lexington Books.

Greer, G. (1971), *The Female Eunuch*, London, Paladin.

Griffin, K. B. (1978), *International Inequality and National Poverty*, New York, Holmes & Meier.

Hacker, S. L. (1981), 'The culture of engineering: woman, workplace and machine', *Women's Studies International Quarterly*, vol. 4, no. 3, pp. 341–53.

Hage, P. (1981), 'On male initiation and dual organisation in New Guinea', *Man: The Journal of the Royal Anthropological Institute*, vol. 16, no. 2, pp. 268–75.

Hall, C. (1980), 'The history of the housewife', in E. Malos (ed.), *The Politics of Housework*, London, Allison & Busby, pp. 44–71.

Haq, M. (1976), *The Poverty Curtain*, New York, Columbia University Press.

Haraway, D. (1978), 'Animal sociology and a natural economy of the body politic, Part I and Part II', *Signs*, vol. 4, no. 1, pp. 21–36, 37–60.

Harrington, M. (1969), *The Other America: Poverty in the United States*, New York, Macmillan.

Harrington, M. (1977), *The Vast Majority: A Journey to the World's Poor*, New York, Simon & Schuster.

Harris, M. (1981), *America Now: the Anthropology of a Changing Culture*, New York, Simon & Schuster.

Hartmann, H. (1980), 'Capitalism, patriarchy, and job segregation by sex', in M. Blaxall and B. Reagan (eds), *Women and the Workplace*, Chicago, University of Chicago Press, pp. 137–69.

Hartmann, H. (1981a), 'The family as the locus of gender, class, and political struggle: the example of housework', *Signs*, vol. 6, no. 3, pp. 366–94.

Hartmann, H. (1981b), 'The unhappy marriage of marxism and feminism: towards a more progressive union?', in L. Sargent (ed.), *Women and Revolution*, Boston, South End Press, pp. 1–41.

Hay, D. (1965), *The Medieval Centuries*, London, Methuen.

Henderson, H. (1978), *Creating Alternative Futures*, New York, Berkley Publishing.

Henderson, H. (1981), *The Politics of the Solar Age*, New York, Anchor Press.

Herlihy, D. (1971), *Women in Medieval Society*, the Smith History Lecture, Houston, University of St Thomas Press.

Herlihy, D. (1976), 'Land, family, and women in continental Europe, 701–1200', in S. M. Stuard (ed.), *Women in Medieval Society*, Philadelphia, University of Pennsylvania Press, pp. 13–45.

Hobsbawm, E. J. (1968), 'Poverty', *International Encyclopedia of the Social Sciences*, New York, Macmillan and the Free Press, pp. 398–404.

Holter, H. and Henriksen, H. V. (1979), 'Social policy and the family in Norway', in J. Lipman-Blumen and J. Bernard (eds), *Sex Roles and Social Policy*, London and Beverly Hills, Sage Publications.

Horney, K. (1926), 'The flight from womanhood', *International Journal of Psychoanalysis*, vol. 7, pp. 324–39.

Hosken, F. P. (1979), *The Hosken Report: Genital and Sexual Mutilation of Females*, Lexington, Mass., Women's International Network News.

Hubbard R. (1979), 'Reflections on the story of the double helix', *Women's Studies International Quarterly*, vol. 2, no. 3, pp. 261–74.

Hubbard, R. and Lowe, M. (eds) (1979), *Genes and Gender II: Pitfalls in Research on Sex and Gender*, New York, Gordian Press.

Huber, J. (ed.) (1973), *Changing Women in a Changing Society*, Chicago, University of Chicago Press.

Iglitzin, L. B. and Ross, R. R. (eds) (1976), *Women in the World*, Santa Barbara, Cal., Clio Press.

International Labor Organization (1981), 'Women, technology and the development process', in R. Dauber and M. L. Cain (eds), *Women and Technological Change in Developing Countries*, Boulder, Col., Westview Press.

Janeway, E. (1980), 'Who is Sylvia? On the loss of sexual paradigms', *Signs*, vol. 5, no. 4, pp. 573–89.

Janjic, M. (1983), 'Women and labor market policy: an overview from ILO perspective', paper presented at Women and Labor Market Policy Conference.

Jelin, E. (1977), 'Migration and labor force participation of Latin American women', *Signs*, vol. 3, no. 1, pp. 129–41.

Johnson, A. G. (1980), 'On the prevalence of rape in the United States', *Signs*, vol. 6, no. 1, pp. 136–46.

Jordanova, L. J. (1980), 'Natural facts: a historical perspective on science and sexuality', in C. MacCormack and M. Strathern (eds), *Nature, Culture and Gender*, Cambridge, New York and Melbourne, Cambridge University Press, pp. 42–69.

Jules-Rosette, B. (1982), 'Women and technological change in the urban informal economy', *Resources for Feminist Research*, vol. 11, no. 1, pp. 37–41.

Kamerman, S. (1982), 'Reagan's mixed message', *Working Woman*, vol. 4, no. 9, p. 90.

Keller, E. F. (1982), 'Feminism and science', *Signs*, vol. 7, no. 3, pp. 589–602.

Kelly, A. and Weinreich-Haste, H. (1979), 'Science is for girls', *Women's Studies International Quarterly*, vol. 2, no. 3, pp. 275–94.

Kessler-Harris, A. (1981), *Women Have Always Worked*, New York, Feminist Press, McGraw Hill.

Klemesrud, J. (1981), 'Conflicts of women with jobs', *The New York Times*, 7 May, pp. C1, C6.

Kneerim, J. and Shur, J. (eds) (n.d.), *The Exchange Report: Women in the Third World*, New York, the Exchange.

Kohlstedt, S. G. (1978), 'In from the periphery: American women in science, 1830–1880', *Signs*, vol. 4, no. 1, pp. 126–35.

Kuhn, A. and Wolpe, A. (eds) (1978), *Feminism and Materialism: Women and Modes of Production*, London, Boston and Melbourne, Routledge & Kegan Paul.

La Fontaine, J. S. (1981), 'The domestication of the savage male', *Man: The Journal of the Royal Anthropological Institute*, vol. 16, no. 3, pp. 333–49.

Lagergren, M. (1983), 'What is happening to care in society?', *Current Sweden*, no. 308, Stockholm, the Swedish Institute.

Lambert, H. H. (1978), 'Biology and equality: a perspective on sex differences', *Signs*, vol. 4, no. 1, pp. 97–117.

Lapidus, G. W. (1978), *Women in the Soviet Union: Equality, Development and Social Change*, Berkeley, University of California Press.

Lapidus, G. W. (1980), 'Occupational segregation and public policy: a comparative analysis of American and Soviet patterns', in M. Blaxall and B. Reagan (eds), *Women and the Workplace*, Chicago, University of Chicago Press, pp. 119–36.

Leacock, E. B. (1981a), *Myths of Male Dominance*, New York, Monthly Review Press.

Leacock, E. B. (1981b), 'History, development, and the division of labor by sex', *Signs*, vol. 7, no. 2, pp. 474–91.

Leibell, H. D. (1971), *Anglo-Saxon Education of Women*, New York, Burt Franklin.

Leighton, L. and Gustafsson, S. (n.d.), 'Differential patterns of unemployment in Sweden', Center for Working Life, Stockholm, unpublished manuscript.

Leira, A. (1983), 'The organization of care-giving work in the welfare state: an illustration of non-market work', *Women and the Labour Market, Research Newsletter*, no. 6, Copenhagen, Women's Research Centre in Social Science, pp. 6–10.

Lenin, V. I. (1952 edn), 'A great beginning', in *Selected Works*, vol. 2, part 2, Moscow, Foreign Languages Publishing House, pp. 213–39.

Lim, L. Y. C. (1981), 'Women's work in multinational electronics factories', in R. Dauber and M. L. Cain (eds), *Women and Technological Change in Developing Countries*, Boulder, Col., Westview Press.

Lipman-Blumen, J. and Bernard, J. (eds) (1979), *Sex Roles and Social Policy*, London and Beverly Hills, Sage Publications.

Little, K. (1976), 'Women in African towns south of the Sahara: the urbanization dilemma', in I. Tinker and M. B. Bramsen (eds), *Women and World Development*, Washington, DC, Overseas Development Council, pp. 78–87.

McAuley, A. (1981), *Women's Work and Wages in the Soviet Union*, London, George Allen & Unwin.

MacCormack, C. and Strathern, M. (eds) (1980), *Nature, Culture and Gender*, Cambridge, New York and Melbourne, Cambridge University Press.

McCrae, J. (1983), 'The socioeconomic status of women in Israel's kibbutzim', paper presented at the meeting of the Eastern Economic Association.

Macdonald, D. (1963), 'Our invisible poor', *The New Yorker*, 19 January, pp. 82–132.

McDonough, R. and Harrison, R. (1978), 'Patriarchy and relations of production', in A. Kuhn and A. Wolpe (eds), *Feminism and Materialism*, London, Boston and Melbourne, Routledge & Kegan Paul, pp. 11–41.

MacKinnon, C. A. (1982), 'Feminism, marxism, method and the state: an agenda for theory', *Signs*, vol. 7, no. 3, pp. 515–44.

Mackintosh, M. (1981), 'Gender and economics: the sexual division of labour and the subordination of women', in K. Young, C. Wolkowitz and R. McCullagh (eds), *Of Marriage and the Market*, London, CSE Books, pp. 1–15. New edition (1984), London, Boston and Melbourne, Routledge & Kegan Paul.

MacLennan, E. (1980), *Minimum Wages for Women*, Manchester, Equal Opportunities Commission.

McNamara, J. and Wemple, S. (1977), 'Sanctity and power: the dual pursuit of medieval women', in R. Bridenthal and C. Koonz (eds), *Becoming Visible: Women in European History*, Boston and London, Houghton Mifflin, pp. 90–118.

Magner, L. N. (1978), 'Women and the scientific idiom: textual episodes from Wollstonecraft, Fuller, Gilman and Firestone', *Signs*, vol. 4, no. 1, pp. 61–80.

Mahoney, P. (1982), ' "Silence is a woman's glory": the sexist content of education', *Women's Studies International Forum*, vol. 5, no. 4, pp. 463–74.

Malos, E. (ed.) (1980), *The Politics of Housework*, London, Allison & Busby.

Malson, M. (1982), 'Black women and white women in the labor force', *Research Report*, Wellesley College Center for Research on Women, vol. 11, no. 1, p. 4.

Marcuse, H. (1972), *Counterrevolution and Revolt*, Boston, Beacon Press.

Martin, B. R. and Irvine, J. (1982), 'Women in science – the astronomical brain drain', *Women's Studies International Forum*, vol. 5, no. 1, pp. 41–68.

Marx, K. (1936 edn), *Capital*, New York, Modern Library.

Marx, K. (1975 edn), 'Economic and philosophical manuscripts' (1844), in *Early Writings*, Harmondsworth, Penguin Books, pp. 279–400.

Marx, K. and Engels, F. (1935 edn), 'The Communist Manifesto', in *A Handbook of Marxism*, New York, International Publishers, pp. 21–59.

Marx, K. and Engels, F. (1953 edn), *On Britain*, Moscow, Foreign Languages Publishing House.

Mason, J. and Blue, P. (1982), 'Getting off welfare: how one family broke the poverty cycle', *Life*, vol. 5, no. 6, pp. 88–98.

Meek, R. L. (1967), *Economics and Ideology and Other Essays: Studies in the Development of Economic Thought*, London, Chapman & Hall.

Merchant, C. (1980), *The Death of Nature: Women, Ecology and the Scientific Revolution*, New York, Harper & Row.

Merkl, P. H. (1976), 'The politics of sex: West Germany', in L. B. Iglitzin and R. R. Ross (eds), *Women in the World*, Santa Barbara, Cal., Clio Press, pp. 129–48.

Mernissi, F. (1976), 'The Moslem world: women excluded from development', in I. Tinker and M. B. Bramsen (eds), *Women and Development*, Washington, DC, Overseas Development Council, pp. 35–44.

Merritt, G. (1982), *World Out of Work*, London, Collins.

Miles, A. (1981), 'The integrative principle in North American feminist radicalism: value basis of a new feminism', *Women's Studies International Quarterly*, vol. 4, no. 4, pp. 481–95.

Miller, S. M. and Roby, P. A. (1970), *The Future of Inequality*, New York, Basic Books.

Millett, K. (1970), *Sexual Politics*, New York, Doubleday.

Minces, J. (1980), *La femme dans le monde arabe*, Paris, Mazarine.

Mitchell, J. (1971), *Woman's Estate*, Harmondsworth, Penguin Books.

Mitchell, J. (1975), *Psychoanalysis and Feminism*, Harmondsworth, Penguin Books.

Morton, A. L. (1957), *A People's History of England*, London, Lawrence & Wishart.

Mueller, M. (1977), 'Women and men, power and powerlessness in Lesotho', *Signs*, vol. 3, no. 1, pp. 154–66.

Münster, A.-M. (n.d.), 'Über Löhne und Subsidien in der Freien Produktionszone Penang/Malaysia', Starnberg, Max Planck Institute, unpublished manuscript.

Myrdal, G. (1973), *Against the Stream*, New York, Pantheon Books.

Nash, J. (1978), 'The ideology of male dominance', *Signs*, vol. 4, no. 2, pp. 349–62.

National Council for One Parent Families (1981), *One Parent Families, Annual Report and Accounts 1980–1981*, London.

Newland, K. (1979), *The Sisterhood of Man*, New York, W. W. Norton.

Newland, K. (1980), *Women, Men, and the Division of Labor*, Washington, DC, Worldwatch Institute, paper no. 37.

Newland, K. (1981), *Infant Mortality and the Health of Societies*, Washington, DC, Worldwatch Institute, paper no. 47.

Nieves, I. (1979), 'Household arrangement and multiple jobs in San Salvador', *Signs*, vol. 5, no. 1, pp. 134–42.

Oakley, A. (1974), *Housewife*, London, Allen Lane.

Oakley, A. (1981), *Subject Women*, New York, Pantheon.

OECD Observer (1980), 'Women in the labour market', no. 104, pp. 3–15.

OECD Observer (1981), 'Youth unemployment', no. 109, pp. 25–31.

OECD Observer (1982), '28½ million unemployed', no. 115, pp. 8–16.

Ortner, S. B. (1974), 'Is female to male as nature is to culture?', in M. Z. Rosaldo and L. Lamphere (eds), *Woman, Culture and Society*, Stanford, Stanford University Press, pp. 67–87.

Papanek, H. (1977), 'Development planning for women', *Signs*, vol. 3, no. 1, pp. 14–21.

Parker, R. (1975), *The Common Stream: Portrait of an English Village Through 2,000 Years*, New York, Holt, Rinehart & Winston.

Patai, R. (ed.) (1967), *Women in the Modern World*, New York, Free Press.

Pearce, D. and McAdoo, H. (1981), *Women and Children: Alone and in Poverty*, Washington, DC, Center for National Policy Review.

Person, E. S. (1980), 'Sexuality as the mainstay of identity: psychoanalytic perspectives', *Signs*, vol. 5, no. 4, pp. 605–30.

Piven, F. F. and Cloward, R. S. (1982), *The New Class War: Reagan's Attack on the Welfare State and its Consequences*, New York, Pantheon Books.

Poewe, K. O. (1980), 'Universal male dominance: an ethnological illusion', *Dialectical Anthropology*, vol. 5, no. 2, pp. 111–25.

Powers, M. N. (1980), 'Menstruation and reproduction: an Oglala case', *Signs*, vol. 6, no. 1, pp. 54–60.

Rapp, R. (1979), 'Review essay: anthropology', *Signs*, vol. 4, no. 3, pp. 497–513.

Raspberry, W. (1983), 'A fair share for a former wife', *Boston Globe*, 18 July.

Reiter, R. R. (ed.) (1975), *Toward an Anthropology of Women*, New York, Monthly Review Press.

Rendel, M. (ed.) (1981), *Women, Power and Political Systems*, London, Croom Helm.

Rich, A. (1980), 'Compulsory heterosexuality and lesbian experience', *Signs*, vol. 5, no. 4, pp. 631–60.

Robertson, J. (1981), 'The future of work: some thoughts about the roles of men and women in the transition to a SHE future', *Women's Studies International Quarterly*, vol. 4, no. 1, pp. 83–94.

Robinson, J. (1968), *Economic Philosophy*, Harmondsworth, Penguin Books.

Robinson, J. (1981), *What are the Questions? Further Contributions to Modern Economics*, Armonk, New York, M. E. Sharpe.

Roll, E. (1939), *A History of Economic Thought*, Englewood Cliffs, New Jersey, Prentice Hall.

Rosaldo, M. Z. (1974), 'Women, culture and society: a theoretical overview', in M. Z. Rosaldo and L. Lamphere (eds), *Women, Culture and Society*, Stanford, Stanford University Press, pp. 17–42.

Rosaldo, M. Z. (1980), 'The use and abuse of anthropology: reflections on feminism and cross-cultural understanding', *Signs*, vol. 5, no. 3, pp. 389–417.

Rosaldo, M. Z. and Lamphere, L. (eds) (1974), *Women, Culture and Society*, Stanford, Stanford University Press.

Rothschild, J. (1981), 'Technology, "women's work" and the social control of women', in M. Rendel (ed.), *Women, Power and Political Systems*, London, Croom Helm, pp. 160–83.

Rowbotham, S. (1972), *Women, Resistance and Revolution*, London, Allen Lane.

Rowbotham, S. (1973), *Hidden from History*, London, Pluto Press.

Safa, H. (1981), 'Runaway shops and female employment: the search for cheap labor', *Signs*, vol. 7, no. 2, pp. 418–33.

Sanday, P. R. (1981), *Female Power and Male Dominance: On the Origins of Sexual Inequality*, Cambridge, New York and Melbourne, Cambridge University Press.

Sargent, L. (ed.) (1981), *Women and Revolution*, Boston, South End Press.

Sawhill, I. (1980), 'Discrimination and poverty among women who head families', in M. Blaxall and B. Reagan (eds), *Women and the Workplace*, Chicago, University of Chicago Press, pp. 201–12.

Sayers, J. (1982), 'My mother, myself: on object relations theory', unpublished manuscript.

Schumacher, E. F. (1973), *Small is Beautiful: Economics as if People Mattered*, New York, Harper & Row.

Scott, H. (1974), *Does Socialism Liberate Women?*, Boston, Beacon Press.

Scott, H. (1982a), *Sweden's "Right to be Human": Sex-Role Equality, the Goal and the Reality*, Armonk, New York, M. E. Sharpe.

Scott, H. (1982b), 'Equality Swedish style', *Working Woman*, June, pp. 21–2.

Scott, H. (1982c), 'Why the revolution doesn't solve everything: what we can learn from the economics of "real" socialism', *Women's Studies International Forum*, vol. 5, no. 5, pp. 451–62.

Scott, J. W. (1982), 'The mechanization of women's work', *Scientific American*, vol. 247, no. 3, pp. 166–87.

Seccombe, W. (1974), 'The housewife and her labour under capitalism', *New Left Review*, no. 83, pp. 3–24.

Shaffer, H. G. (1981), *Women in the Two Germanies: A Comparative Study of a Socialist and a Non-Socialist Society*, New York, Oxford, Pergamon Press.

Shannon, C. and Henwood, F. (1982), 'Technology and women's employment', *Women and the Labour Market, Research Newsletter*, no. 5, Copenhagen, Women's Research Centre in Social Science, pp. 6–11.

Shulman, A. K. (1980), 'Sex and power: sexual bases of radical feminism', *Signs*, vol. 5, no. 4, pp. 590–604.

Sivard, R. L. (1982), *World Military and Social Expenditures*, Leesburg, Va., World Priorities.

Skar, S. L. (1979), 'The use of the public/private framework in the analysis of egalitarian societies', *Women's Studies International Quarterly*, vol. 2, no. 4, pp. 449–60.

Smith, A. (1937 edn), *The Wealth of Nations*, New York, Modern Library, p. 241.

Smith, P. (1978), 'Domestic labour and Marx's theory of value', in A. Kuhn and A. Wolpe (eds), *Feminism and Materialism*, London, Boston and Melbourne, Routledge & Kegan Paul, pp. 198–219.

Sokoloff, N. J. (1980), *Between Money and Love: The Dialectics of Women's Home and Market Work*, New York, Praeger.

Solman, P. and Friedman, T. (1982), *Life and Death on the Corporate Battlefield*, New York, Simon & Schuster.

Spender, D. (1982), *Invisible Women: The Schooling Scandal*, London, Readers & Writers Cooperative.

Stanley, A. (1981), 'Daughters of Isis, daughters of Demeter: when women sowed and reaped', *Women's Studies International Quarterly*, vol. 4, no. 3, pp. 289–304.

Stanworth, M. (1983), *Gender and Schooling*, London, Hutchinson.

Steedman, I., Sweezy, P. *et al.* (1981), *The Value Controversy*, London, Verso Editions.

Stephenson, C. (1982), 'Feminism, nationalism, pacifism, and the United Nations Decade for Women', *Women's Studies International Forum*, vol. 5, nos. 3–4, pp. 287–300.

Stern, G. (1979), *Israeli Women Speak Out*, New York, J. B. Lippincott.

Stoler, A. (1977), 'Class structure and female autonomy in rural Java', *Signs*, vol. 3, no. 1, pp. 77–89.

Strachey, R. (1930), *Struggle*, New York, Duffield.

Strathern, M. (1980), 'No nature, no culture: the Hagen case', in C. MacCormack and M. Strathern (eds), *Nature, Culture and Gender*, Cambridge, New York and Melbourne, Cambridge University Press, pp. 174–222.

Strathern, M. (1981), 'Culture in a net bag: the manufacture of a subdiscipline in anthropology', *Man: The Journal of the Royal Anthropological Institute*, vol. 16, no. 4, pp. 665–88.

Strober, M. H. (1976), 'Women and men in the world of work: present and future', in L. A. Cater and A. F. Scott (eds), *Women and Men: Changing Roles, Relationships and Perceptions*, New York, Aspen Institute, pp. 119–52.

Stuard, S. M. (ed.) (1976), *Women in Medieval Society*, Philadelphia, University of Pennsylvania Press.

Stuckey, B. and Fay, M. A. (1980), 'Rural subsistence, migration, and urbanization: the production, destruction, and reproduction of cheap labour in the world market economy', Starnberg, Max-Planck-Institute, unpublished manuscript. (Published in German in 1980 in *Starnberger Studien 4 – Strukturveränderungen in der kapitalistischen Weltwirtschaft*, Frankfurt, edition suhrkamp 982.)

Sullerot, E. (1976), *Women, Society and Change*, New York and Toronto, McGraw Hill.

Szalai, S. (1976), 'Women in the light of time–budget research', *New Hungarian Quarterly*, vol. 17, no. 64, pp. 74–92.

Tadesse, Z. (1982), 'Women and technology in peripheral countries: an overview', in P. M. D'Onofrio-Flores and S. M. Pfafflin (eds), *Scientific–Technological Change and the Role of Women in Development*, Boulder, Col., Westview Press, pp. 77–112.

Tanner, N. and Zihlman, A. (1976), 'Women in evolution, part I: innovation and selection in human origins', *Signs*, vol. 1, no. 3, pp. 585–608.

Thönnessen, W. (1973), *The Emancipation of Women: The Rise and Decline of the Women's Movement in German Social Democracy 1863–1933*, London, Pluto Press.

Tilly, L. A. and Scott, J. W. (1978), *Women, Work and Family*, New York, Holt, Rinehart & Winston.

Tinker, I. (1976), 'The adverse impact of development on women', in I. Tinker and M. B. Bramsen (eds), *Women and World Development*, Washington, DC, Overseas Development Council.

Tinker, I. (1981), 'International notes: a feminist view of Copenhagen', *Signs*, vol. 6, no. 3, pp. 531–35.

Tinker, I. and Bramsen, M. B. (eds) (1976), *Women and World Development*, Washington, DC, Overseas Development Council.

Titmuss, R. M. (1962), *Income Distribution and Social Change*, London, George Allen & Unwin.

Townsend, P. (1979), *Poverty in the UK*, Berkeley, University of California Press.

Turnbull, C. (1981), 'Mbuti womanhood', in F. Dahlberg (ed.), *Woman the Gatherer*, New Haven and London, Yale University Press, pp. 205–20.

Turner, E. S. (1966), *Roads to Ruin*, Harmondsworth, Penguin Books.

US Dept of Health, Education, and Welfare (1976), *The Measure of Poverty: A Report to Congress as Mandated by the Education Amendments of 1974*, Washington, DC, US Government Printing Office.

United Nations Development Programme (n.d.), 'Women and the new international economic order', *Development Issue Paper for the 1980s*, no. 12, New York UNDP Division of Information.

United Nations Development Programme (n.d.), 'Women and technical co-operation among developing countries', *Development Issue Paper for the 1980s*, no. 13, New York, UNDP Division of Information.

Valentine, C. (1968), *Culture and Poverty*, Chicago, University of Chicago Press.

Varette, S. and Warskett, G. (1981), 'Word processing and office technology', paper presented at Canadian Political Science Association Meeting.

Vavrus, L. G. and Cadieux, R. (1980), *Women in Development: A Selected Annotated Bibliography and Resource Guide*, Non-Formal Education Center, East Lansing, Michigan State University.

Volgyes, I. (1980), 'Blue collar working women and poverty in Hungary', paper presented at Conference on Status of Women in Eastern Europe.

Wadley, S. S. (1977), 'Women and the Hindu tradition', *Signs*, vol. 3, no. 1, pp. 113–25.

Walkowitz, J. R. (1980), 'The politics of prostitution', *Signs*, vol. 6, no. 1, pp. 123–35.

Warskett, G. (1981), 'The choice of technology and women in the paid work force', paper presented at Workshop on Women and the Canadian Labour Force.

Washburn, S. L. and Ranieri, S. (1981), 'Who brought home the bacon?', *New York Review of Books*, 24 September, pp. 59–61.

Watson, J. D. (1968), *The Double Helix*, New York, New American Library.

Weeks, J. (1981), *Politics and Society: The Regulation of Sexuality since 1800*, London, Longmans.

Weinbaum, B. and Bridges, A. (1979), 'The other side of the paycheck: monopoly capital and the structure of consumption', in Z. Eisenstein (ed.), *Capitalism, Patriarchy, and the Case for Socialist Feminism*, New York, Monthly Review Press, pp. 190–205.

Weir, A. and Wilson, E. (1973), 'Women's labor, women's discontent', *Radical America*, vol. 7, nos. 3–4, pp. 80–94.

West, J. (1978), 'Women, sex, and class', in A. Kuhn and A. Wolpe (eds), *Feminism and Materialism*, London, Boston and Melbourne, Routledge & Kegan Paul, pp. 220–53.

Wilson, E. (1981), 'Psychoanalysis: psychic law and order?', *Feminist Review*, no. 8, pp. 63–78.

Wistrand, B. (1981), *Swedish Women on the Move*, Stockholm, the Swedish Institute.

Women at Work (1982), 'Households headed by women', Geneva, International Labor Organization, pp. 11–12.

Young, K., Wolkowitz, C. and McCullagh, R. (eds) (1981), *Of Marriage and the Market: Women's Subordination in International Perspective*, London, CSE Books. New edition (1984), London, Boston and Melbourne, Routledge & Kegan Paul.

Youssef, N. H. (1976), 'Women in development: urban life and labor', in I. Tinker and M. B. Bramsen (eds), *Women and Development*, Washington, DC, Overseas Development Council, pp. 70–7.

Youssef, N. H. (1977), *Women and Work in Developing Societies*, Westport, Conn., Greenwood Press.

Zihlman, A. L. (1978), 'Women in evolution, part II: subsistence and social organization among early hominids', *Signs*, vol. 4, no. 1, pp. 4–20.

Zihlman, A. L. (1981), 'Women as shapers of the human adaptation', in F. Dahlberg (ed.), *Woman the Gatherer*, New Haven and London, Yale University Press, pp. 75–120.

Zimmerman, J. (1981), 'Technology and the future of women: haven't we met somewhere before?', *Women's Studies International Quarterly*, vol. 4, no. 3, pp. 355–68.

INDEX

P A N D O R A P R E S S

an imprint of Routledge and Kegan Paul

Some Pandora titles you may enjoy:

WOMEN'S HISTORY IN SHORT STORIES

the companion volume to Old Maids

DARING TO DREAM

Utopian stories by United States women: 1836-1919

Carol Farley Kessler

Carol Farley Kessler has unearthed an extraordinary assortment of visionary writing, writings which encapsulate all the yearnings of a vanished generation for a future which has still to be made. Some women write with irony, describing journeys through time and space to parallel but inverted worlds where sober-suited women run commerce and affairs of state while men either prink and preen in beribboned breeches, or are weakened by the burden of unending housework. Other writers lay out complicated blueprints for a non-sexist society. One woman dreams, touchingly, of a fantastic future where men get up in the night to comfort crying children. The stories demonstrate that even in the early nineteenth century women were arguing that male and female 'character traits' were the product of their roles, not of their biology; and they make apparent the hidden roots of the discontent, longing and anger which was later to erupt in the great movements of women for change.

0-86358-013-0 Fiction/Social History 256pp 198 × 129 mm paperback

ELIZABETH GASKELL : FOUR SHORT STORIES

The Three Eras of Libbie Marsh · Lizzie Leigh · The Well of Pen-Morfa · The Manchester Marriage

In her unaffected, direct description of the lives of working class women as lived out between the mean streets and the cotton mills of nineteenth century England, Elizabeth Gaskell chose to break with the literary conventions of Victorian ladies' fiction (which demanded genteel romances) and give her readers, instead, the harsh realities, the defiance and courage those lives entailed. Far from being delicate drawing room flowers, the characters in these four stories (collected here for the first time) are women who live unsupported by men, who labour and love and scheme and survive in strangely modern tales shot through with Gaskell's integrity of observation and deep compassion. The stories are prefaced by a long appreciation of Gaskell's life and work by Anna Walters.

'Mrs Gaskell draws the distinction between male and female values quietly, but forcefully'   *School Librarian*

0-86358-001-7 Fiction/Criticism 122pp 198 × 129 mm introduced by Anna Walters paperback.

DISCOVERING WOMEN'S HISTORY

a practical manual

Deirdre Beddoe

Rainy Sunday afternoons, long winter evenings: why not set yourself a research project, either on your own or in a group or classroom? This is the message from Deirdre Beddoe, an historian who tears away the mystique of her own profession in this step-by-step guide to researching the lives of ordinary women in Britain from 1800 to 1945. *Discovering Women's History* tells you how to get started on the detective trail of history and how to stalk your quarry through attics and art galleries, museums and old newspapers, church archives and the Public Records Office – and how to publish your findings once you have completed your project.

'an invaluable and fascinating guide to the raw material for anyone approaching this unexplored territory'   *The Sunday Times*

'Thrilling and rewarding and jolly good fun'   *South Wales Argus*

0-86358-008-4 Hobbies/Social History 232pp 198 × 129 mm illustrated

ALL THE BRAVE PROMISES

Memories of Aircraftwomen 2nd Class 2146391

Mary Lee Settle

Mary Lee Settle was a young American woman living a comfortable life in Washington D.C. when the Second World War broke out. In 1942 she boarded a train, carrying 'a last bottle of champagne and an armful of roses', and left for England to join the WAAF. She witnessed the horror of war – the bombing raids, the planes lost in fog, the children evacuated, a blacked-out Britain of austerity and strain. She also witnessed the women, her fellow recruits, as they struggled to adapt to their new identities and new lives at the bottom of the uniformed pile. Dedicated 'to the wartime other ranks of the Women's Auxiliary Air Force – below the rank of Sergeant', this rare book captures women's wartime experience; a remarkable and important story by one of America's prizewinning novelists.

'One of the most moving accounts of war experience ever encountered' *Library Journal*

0-86358-033-5 General/Autobiography 160pp 198 × 129 mm paperback

not for sale in the U.S.A. or Canada

MY COUNTRY IS THE WHOLE WORLD

an anthology of women's work on peace and war

Cambridge Women's Peace Collective (eds)

Women's struggle for peace is no recent phenomenon. In this book, the work of women for peace from 600 BC to the present is documented in a unique collection of extracts from songs, poems, diaries, letters, petitions, pictures, photographs and pamphlets through the ages. A book to give as a gift, to read aloud from, to research from, to teach from, *My Country is the Whole World* is both a resource and an inspiration for all who work for peace today.

'an historic document . . . readers will be amazed at the extent of the collection' *Labour Herald*

'a beautifully presented and illustrated book which makes for accessible and enlightening reading' *Morning Star*

0-86358-004-1 Social Questions/History 306pp A5 illustrated throughout paperback